Chicken! Chicken! Chicken!
and More Chicken!

Chicken! Chicken! Chicken! and More Chicken!

Lynn Mendelson

WHITECAP BOOKS
VANCOUVER/TORONTO

The information in this book is true and complete to the best of our knowledge. The author and publisher disclaim any liability in connection with the use of this information. For additional information, please contact Whitecap Books, 351 Lynn Avenue, North Vancouver, BC V7J 2C4.

Edited by Elizabeth McLean
Proofread by Kathy Evans
Interior design by Warren Clark
Cover design by Warren Clark
Cover illustration by Guy Buffet
Print of illustration photographed by Robert Keziere

Printed and bound in Canada

Canadian Cataloguing in Publication Data

Mendelson, Lynn, 1952–
    Chicken! chicken! chicken! and more chicken!

    Includes index
    ISBN 1-55285-015-3

    1. Cookery (Chicken) I. Title.
TX750.5.C45M45 2000   641.6'65   C00-910073-3

The publisher acknowledges the support of the Canada Council for the Arts and the Cultural Services Branch of the Government of British Columbia for our publishing program. We acknowledge the financial support of the Government of Canada through the Book Industry Development Program for our publishing activities.

Contents

Foreword

The rising popularity of chicken comes as no surprise. It is nutritious, tasty and versatile—a very suitable match for today's busy consumer. Chicken (without the skin) is low in fat and high in protein. The flavor of chicken wonderfully complements a great variety of vegetables, fruits and grains. Dietitians have been encouraging people to eat more of these foods for years and for good reason. Chicken suits the tastes of even the most picky eaters and appeals to young and old alike, blending easily with such diverse leaves as cilantro and basil or fruits as different as apricots and tomatoes.

In addition to all of these great attributes, chicken is economical, yet neutral in status. Guests will never feel shortchanged by a homemade chicken dinner. Without financial pressure, a clever cook can add elegance to any table featuring the recipes in this book. Most of the recipes can be adapted to serve one person or a crowd.

Lynn Mendelson's resurrection of her runaway bestseller comes at a perfect time, when so many cooks are asking for more ideas to prepare chicken for their families and guests.

—Rena Mendelson

Acknowledgments

With thanks to mother Roz, sisters Rena, Susan and Anita, brother Fred, Deborah Roitberg, Audrey Ellison, Marilyn and Arthur Zivian, Louise Shalit, Michiko Sakata, John Disney, Mary Ambrose, Zonda Nellis, Sheri Brautigam, Anne Henry, Lorene Vickberg, Wild Wilbur, Gail Posluns, Sandy Posluns, Lyla Soloman, Doreen Levine, Richard Weiss, Andrea Bronstein, Charlotte Odele, Karen Levine, Danny Cushing, Mrs. Robinson, Leslie Grant, Barbara Cohen, Jack Amar, Peter Cassidy, Matti, Agathe Simard, Susan Yorke, Margie Shore, Sheila Barrazuol, Leora MacDonald, Nancy Adelman, Delia Gayo, Zenaida Bonagua, the smiling faces at Vanipha Lanna who taught me that food has to appeal to all the senses to taste good, the discerning clients of Lynn Mendelson Catering and all the friendly faces at The Lazy Gourmet.

With special thanks to David Robinson, who was my typist, editor, publisher and friend during the first edition.

With appreciation for the support and encouragement of Jennifer Grange of The Cookbook Store in Toronto who remembered *Chicken! Chicken! Chicken!* after all these years.

With a hug and a kiss to my children Joanna, Andrea, Rochelle and Nathaniel, who will someday be willing to try more of these recipes.

And, finally, with love and thanks to my husband and best friend, Ira Basen, to whom this book is dedicated.

David Robinson would like to thank Zonda Nellis and Michael Burch (once again); and special thanks to Mario Enero for finding us the cover silkscreen, and to Marian Babchuk for owning a copy.

Introduction

"What a great idea for a book!" That was the first reaction from just about everybody I talked to about my plan to write a cookbook consisting exclusively of chicken recipes.

That was (gulp!) fifteen years ago. There weren't a lot of chicken cookbooks on the market at that time, and the cookbook quickly became a bestseller. Since then, I've had four children and started a successful catering business where I serve a lot of—wait for it...chicken.

In my introduction to the original edition of *Chicken! Chicken! Chicken!*, I boldly proclaimed chicken to be the "dish of the '80s." Well here we are in the '00s, and I'm standing by my original statement. Chicken consumption continues to grow... up to 55 pounds (25 kilograms) a year for the average Canadian.

Eating chicken will generally cost you less than eating meat, and it's better for you. It is lower in cholesterol, calories and fat than even the leanest, most expensive cuts of red meat.

My own love affair with the fabulous fowl dates back to my earliest childhood memories. My parents, faced with the unenviable task of driving across Canada in a car with four unruly children, would try to buy a few hours of peace in the morning by promising us that, if we kept quiet, we could order whatever we wanted to eat at the first pit stop. It was then, somewhere in the middle of Manitoba, at 9 a.m., that I discovered fried chicken and I have been quiet ever since!

Chicken continued to be part of my life, as I grew up in a traditional Jewish household in Toronto where chicken was served every Friday night. One of the joys of leaving home was the realization that I could eat chicken on other nights besides Friday. What a sense of liberation that was to this chicken-lover! Chicken every night of the week!

My knowledge of the bird expanded when I went to college. Chicken was the perfect food for the busy student. It was easy to prepare and it was easy on the budget. Some say I spent more time in the kitchen than I did in the classroom—but, what the hey, I got my degree! I got a job! Over the years, my admiration for chicken has grown. I have explored what other nationalities have done with chicken and, in this book, I'm sharing my knowledge with you.

In preparing this edition of *Chicken! Chicken! Chicken!*, I realized that a lot has changed in 15 years. For one thing, I've been exposed to all kinds of new ideas for cooking chicken. And many recipes that seemed good back in the '80s no longer seem so appealing in the more health-conscious world of the new millennium. So in this edition, old standards like Waldorf salad are gone and exciting new recipes like Grilled Chicken with Norigama Sauce have been added.

I hope you'll try them all. Enjoy!

Lynn Mendelson
Toronto

Nibbles

Appetizers are an integral part of contemporary entertaining. Sometimes they introduce the meal, but other times, when served in variety and quantity, they can substitute for the meal itself.

This chapter includes some of my favorite hot and cold hors d'oeuvres. Some can be prepared ahead of time, like the Fritters and Spring Rolls; others, like the Yakitori and dolmades, have to be prepared at the last minute. When organizing your menu, take into account how much time you'll have on the day of your party for last-minute preparation.

And don't forget, if you're having a dinner party—although people love hors d'oeuvres, make sure they leave room for the rest of the meal.

Antipasto

This one marinates overnight!

This antipasto has been a traditional favorite in North America since the sixties. It has stood the test of time and continues to delight at family gatherings in our home. I like that I can make it ahead and check it off my "to do" list before the day of the event.

2	whole chicken breasts, split, skinned and deboned, then cut into bite-size pieces	2
2 Tbsp.	vegetable oil	30 mL
1	12-oz. (340-mL) bottle ketchup	1
1	10-oz. (284-mL) bottle chili sauce	1
1	10-oz. (284-mL) can sliced mushrooms, drained	1
½	14-oz. (398-mL) can artichokes, drained and quartered	½
½	15-oz. (426-mL) jar sweet pickles, with onions and cauliflower, drained, cut into bite-size pieces	½
10–15	pitted, sliced black olives	10–15
2	carrots, peeled and chopped in rounds	2
3	stalks celery, diced	3
3–4	dashes hot pepper sauce	3–4

Sauté chicken in oil in a skillet over medium heat until color becomes opaque, about 6 minutes, then remove from skillet with a slotted spoon and put in a large bowl.

Add remaining ingredients to the chicken and mix together. Put in the refrigerator overnight. It is ready for your guests.

Serve with your favorite crackers. Chicken Antipasto keeps up to 1 week in the refrigerator. I find it gets better as the week goes on!

Cold Chicken Dolmades

Make the dip the night before.

My friend Lorene Vickberg shared this recipe with me. Although the dolmades should be prepared the day of your party, the dip must be prepared a day ahead.

Makes 100

4	whole chicken breasts, split and deboned	4
4 cups	chicken stock (page 32)	1 L
¼ cup	soy sauce	50 mL
2	cloves garlic, minced	2
2	bay leaves	2
1 lb.	washed, stemmed spinach leaves, steamed briefly	500 g
1 recipe	Asian Sour Cream (next page)	1 recipe

Preheat oven to 350°F (180°C).

Put chicken in a 9- x 13-inch (23- x 33-cm) baking dish.

Mix the chicken stock, soy sauce, garlic and bay leaves in a bowl, then pour over chicken in the baking dish.

Bake for 20–25 minutes, until the chicken is cooked completely, then remove dish from oven and allow chicken to cool. Remove skin from chicken and chop chicken into bite-size pieces.

Wrap chicken pieces in spinach leaves and arrange, seam side down, on a serving platter. These can be held together with toothpicks.

Serve with Asian Sour Cream on the side.

Asian Sour Cream

*If you're looking for less fat in your diet, substitute light
sour cream or low-fat plain yogurt.*

1 cup	sour cream	250 mL
¼ cup	soy sauce	50 mL
¼ cup	sesame seeds	50 mL
1	clove garlic, crushed	1
¼ tsp.	minced ginger	1 mL
	white pepper to taste	

Mix all the ingredients in a bowl and chill in the
refrigerator overnight.

Crispy Baked Chicken Fingers

When I wrote the original cookbook in 1985 I was pregnant with my first child. This was the first chicken dish she identified as a favorite. Now I have four children who love this dish.

Makes 24

2	whole chicken breasts, split, skinned and deboned, then cut into long, thin fingers	2
½ cup	tamari sauce	125 mL
¼ cup	dry red wine	50 mL
2 tsp.	sugar	10 mL
¼ tsp.	ground ginger	1 mL
½ cup	fine breadcrumbs	125 mL
½ cup	corn flake crumbs	125 mL
1 tsp.	each finely chopped fresh parsley, basil and thyme	5 mL
½ tsp.	salt	2 mL
¼ cup	melted butter	50 mL
1 recipe	Lazy Plum Sauce (page 7)	1 recipe

Make a marinade by combining the tamari, wine, sugar and ginger in a large bowl. Marinate the chicken for 1 hour in the refrigerator, turning occasionally.

Preheat oven to 400°F (200°C).

Combine the breadcrumbs, corn flakes, parsley, basil, thyme and salt in a bowl. Remove chicken from the marinade and dip in the crumb mixture, then put on a baking sheet.

Sprinkle the melted butter over the chicken. Bake 6–7 minutes per side.

Serve with Lazy Plum Sauce or chutney on the side.

Crispy Fried Chicken Fingers with Lemon-Tamari Sauce

These make a great light meal when served with a crisp tossed green salad. Sometimes when we have guests for dinner, I make a more elaborate dish for the adults and prepare this for the children. I always make extra because the adults want some too.

Serves 4 to 6

2	whole chicken breasts, split, skinned and deboned, then cut into long, thin fingers	2
	juice of 1 lemon	
4 Tbsp.	flour	60 mL
1 tsp.	dried parsley flakes	5 mL
1 tsp.	chopped fresh or dried chives	5 mL
½ tsp.	freshly ground black pepper	2 mL
4 Tbsp.	vegetable oil	60 mL
¼	head iceberg lettuce, shredded	¼
2	green onions, rinsed and chopped	2
1 Tbsp.	toasted sesame seeds	15 mL
1 recipe	Lemon-Tamari Sauce (next page)	1 recipe

Place chicken in a 9-inch (22-cm) square baking dish.

Sprinkle lemon juice over the chicken, cover the baking dish, and put in the refrigerator for 2 hours.

Combine flour, parsley, chives, and pepper in a paper bag.

Shake chicken in the bag until strips are completely covered.

Fry chicken in oil, in a skillet over medium-high heat, for 1–2 minutes on one side, until golden brown. Turn chicken and fry for an additional 30 seconds to 1 minute, then remove from skillet with a slotted spoon and drain on paper towels.

Serve on a bed of lettuce. Garnish with chopped green onions and toasted sesame seeds and serve with Lemon-Tamari Sauce on the side.

TOASTING NUTS AND SEEDS:

To toast sesame seeds, cashews or sunflower seeds I heat a non-stick pan on top of the stove. When it is hot I add the nuts or seeds and toss lightly until they are brown. The nuts and seeds release enough of their own oil to fry in.

Lemon-Tamari Sauce

½ cup	tamari or soy sauce	125 mL
¼ cup	freshly squeezed lemon juice	50 mL
1	clove garlic, crushed	1
1 Tbsp.	sugar	15 mL
1 Tbsp.	sesame oil	15 mL
3	green onions, rinsed and finely chopped	3
1 tsp.	chopped fresh chives	5 mL

Combine all the ingredients in a bowl until the sugar is dissolved.

Lazy Plum Sauce

1 cup	plum preserves	250 mL
½ cup	chutney	125 mL
1 Tbsp.	red wine vinegar	15 mL
2	dashes of hot pepper sauce	2

Thoroughly combine all ingredients in a bowl.

Fritters

These are great for parties because they can be made ahead and frozen. Simply thaw the fritters at room temperature for 1 hour before serving and reheat in a 400°F (200°C) oven.

Serves 4 to 6

6	shallots, thinly sliced	6
2	cloves garlic, minced	2
1 Tbsp.	finely chopped fresh cilantro	15 mL
2 Tbsp.	unsalted butter	30 mL
½ tsp.	salt	2 mL
	freshly ground black pepper to taste	
¼ tsp.	ground nutmeg	1 mL
2	whole chicken breasts, split, skinned and deboned, then chopped	2
2	eggs	2
2 tsp.	cornstarch	10 mL
¼ cup	shelled sunflower seeds	50 mL
¼ cup	toasted cashew pieces (see page 7)	50 mL
	vegetable oil for deep frying	

Sauté shallots, garlic and cilantro in butter in a skillet over medium heat for 2 minutes, then remove from heat.

Purée raw chicken in a food processor or blender. Season with salt, pepper and nutmeg. Add eggs, cornstarch and the shallot mixture to the chicken, and process with 10 on/off pulses.

Add sunflower seeds and cashew pieces and process with 3 on/off pulses.

Pour oil into a skillet to a depth of ½ inch (1 cm) and heat to medium-high, or heat oil in a deep fryer to a temperature of 375°F (190°C). Drop chicken mixture by the spoonful into the skillet and fry for 2–3 minutes per side until browned—or fry in hot oil in a deep fryer until browned. Remove with a slotted spoon and drain on paper towels, then serve.

Oh So Sticky Wings

These wings are sticky, so save them for family gatherings where you can lick your fingers with impunity! Find something else for the night the boss is coming to dinner.

Makes 24

24	chicken wings	24
	salt and freshly ground black pepper to taste	
4 Tbsp.	liquid honey	60 mL
5 Tbsp.	soy sauce	75 mL
5 Tbsp.	brown sugar	75 mL
1 Tbsp.	vegetable oil	15 mL
4-5	cloves garlic, minced	4-5
2 tsp.	minced ginger	10 mL
3-4 Tbsp.	liquid honey	45-60 mL
2 Tbsp.	toasted sesame seeds (see page 7)	30 mL

Preheat oven to 325°F (160°C).

Rinse wings well, then drain on paper towels. Season with salt and pepper.

In a bowl, thoroughly combine 4 Tbsp. (60 mL) honey, soy sauce, brown sugar, oil, garlic and ginger.

Dip wings, a few at a time, into the mixture, then place on a cookie sheet.

Bake for 45 minutes on one side.

Drizzle remaining honey over wings and bake for an additional 30 minutes on same side.

Turn wings over, sprinkle with sesame seeds and bake for 20 minutes more.

Salt and Garlic Wings with Lemon

My friend Michiko shared this recipe with me. It sounds too easy to be delicious. Don't be fooled. Michiko would never steer you wrong.

Makes 24

24	chicken wings	24
3–4 Tbsp.	salt	45–60 mL
6	cloves garlic, minced	6
4	lemons, cut in 6 wedges each	4

Preheat oven to broil or grill.

Rinse wings well, then drain on paper towels. Season with salt, then rub garlic into wings.

Put wings on a baking sheet and place baking sheet in oven, 6 inches (15 cm) from the element. Broil or grill for 10 minutes per side. Do not burn.

Serve with lemon wedges to squeeze over wings before eating.

Honey-Mustard Wings

These spicy wings are sticky, so make sure you have lots of napkins. Better yet, have small bowls of hot water, garnished with lemon, available with the napkins.

Makes 24

24	chicken wings	24
	salt and freshly ground black pepper to taste	
½ cup	liquid honey	125 mL
¼ cup	melted butter	50 mL
5 Tbsp.	Dijon mustard	75 mL
2 Tbsp.	sesame seeds	30 mL

Preheat oven to 325°F (160°C).

Rinse wings well, then drain on paper towels. Season with salt and pepper.

In a bowl, combine honey, butter and mustard.

Dip wings, a few at a time, into the bowl, then place on a baking sheet.

Bake for 45 minutes on one side, basting occasionally with pan juices.

Turn wings over, sprinkle with sesame seeds and bake for an additional 45 minutes, then serve.

Chicken Wings in Beer

These wings look like Oh So Sticky Wings, but they taste quite different! Marinate them overnight for the best flavor.

Makes 24

24	chicken wings	24
¾ cup	orange juice	175 mL
¾ cup	beer	175 mL
¼ cup	vegetable oil	50 mL
¼ cup	brown sugar	50 mL
4	green onions, rinsed and finely chopped	4
2	cloves garlic, crushed	2
2 tsp.	minced ginger	10 mL

Rinse wings well, then drain on paper towels.

Make a marinade by combining the orange juice, beer, oil, brown sugar, green onions, garlic and ginger in a large bowl.

Marinate the wings in the refrigerator overnight.

Preheat oven to 325°F (160°C).

Put wings on a baking sheet and bake for 1½ hours.

Wild Wilbur's Buffalo Wings

Make the Blue Cheese Dip before you prepare the chicken.

T. hese wings are party favorites! **Save the bus fare to Buffalo and make them in your own kitchen.**

Makes 24		
24	chicken wings	24
2 tsp.	onion powder	10 mL
2 tsp.	garlic powder	10 mL
2 tsp.	chili powder	10 mL
2 tsp.	ground cumin	10 mL
2 tsp.	cayenne	10 mL
2 tsp.	salt	10 mL
2 tsp.	freshly ground black pepper	10 mL
¼ cup	melted butter	50 mL
6 Tbsp.	hot pepper sauce	90 mL
	vegetable oil for deep frying	
3	carrots, peeled and cut into sticks	3
3	stalks celery, cut into sticks	3
1 recipe	Blue Cheese Dip (next page)	1 recipe

Rinse wings well, then drain on paper towels.

Combine the onion, garlic and chili powders, cumin, cayenne, salt and pepper in a bowl.

Dredge wings, one at a time, in the seasoning mix.

Pour oil into a skillet to a depth of ½ inch (1 cm) and heat to medium-high—or heat oil in a deep fryer to a temperature of 375°F (190°C). Put wings, a few at a time, in skillet or deep fryer and fry for 15 minutes per batch. Remove from skillet or deep fryer with a slotted spoon and drain on paper towels.

Combine melted butter and hot pepper sauce in a bowl or small saucepan.

Dip wings in butter sauce. Serve with carrot and celery sticks and Blue Cheese Dip on the side.

Blue Cheese Dip

1	egg	1
1 tsp.	dry mustard	5 mL
¾ cup	vegetable oil	175 mL
⅔ cup	crumbled blue cheese	150 mL
2	green onions, rinsed and finely chopped	2
	salt and freshly ground black pepper to taste	

Combine egg and dry mustard in a food processor or blender.

With the motor running, slowly add the oil in a thin, steady stream.

Add blue cheese and green onions and blend in, then refrigerate. Serve at room temperature.

Chinese Wings

These wings are sticky and tasty. If you want them as a meal, serve with rice and stir-fried vegetables. They're simple and your children will eat them without complaints.

Makes 24

24	chicken wings	24
	salt and freshly ground black pepper to taste	
½ cup	liquid honey	125 mL
¼ cup	soy sauce	50 mL
¼ cup	ketchup	50 mL
4 Tbsp.	brown sugar	60 mL
2	cloves garlic, crushed	2
1 tsp.	sesame oil	5 mL

Preheat oven to 375°F (190°C).

Rinse wings well, then drain on paper towels. Season with salt and pepper.

Place wings on a baking sheet. Bake for 45 minutes on one side, then remove the baking sheet from the oven and pour off pan juices.

While the wings are cooking, combine the honey, soy sauce, ketchup, brown sugar, garlic and sesame oil in a bowl.

Turn wings over, pour basting sauce over them, increase heat to 400°F (200°C) and bake for an additional 60 minutes, basting with sauce every 15 minutes.

Pistachio & Chicken Roll

his is delicious for a summer lunch. Serve with a light, green salad on the side and finish the meal with sorbet. Don't forget the mint julep and straw hats.

Serves 4 to 6

2	whole chicken breasts, split, skinned and deboned	2
2 Tbsp.	melted butter	30 mL
	juice of ½ lemon	
3	shallots, finely chopped	3
1	clove garlic, minced	1
3 Tbsp.	unsalted butter	45 mL
2 Tbsp.	flour	30 mL
¼ cup	dry white wine	50 mL
½ cup	milk	125 mL
	salt and freshly ground black pepper to taste	
¼ tsp.	cayenne	1 mL
½ cup	sour cream	125 mL
¼ cup	chopped pistachio nuts	50 mL
20	sheets phyllo pastry (about 1 pkg.), thawed	20
¾ cup	melted butter	175 mL

Preheat oven to 450°F (230°C). Put chicken in a 9-inch (22-cm) square baking dish and brush with 2 Tbsp. (30 mL) melted butter. Sprinkle with lemon juice.

Cover dish with aluminum foil and bake for 8–10 minutes, until chicken is cooked thoroughly. Remove dish from oven, allow chicken to cool, then chop and set aside.

Sauté shallots and garlic in unsalted butter in a skillet over medium heat for 1 minute.

Add flour to the shallot mixture and blend in, stirring constantly for 1 minute.

Slowly add dry white wine and blend in, stirring constantly until mixture has the consistency of a thick paste.

Slowly add milk and blend in, stirring constantly until mixture is thick and smooth.

Season with salt, pepper and cayenne, then remove skillet from heat.

Add sour cream to skillet and blend in.

Add pistachio nuts and chicken to skillet and mix together, then set aside.

Preheat oven to 400°F (200°C).

Put one sheet of phyllo pastry on your work surface and brush with some of the melted butter. Keep remaining pastry covered with a damp cloth to prevent drying.

Layer a few more sheets of pastry, brushing each sheet with melted butter, then put one-quarter of the chicken-pistachio filling along the long edge of the layers of pastry layers, leaving about 2 inches (5 cm) free at each end. Cover with two more sheets of pastry, brushing each with butter.

Roll up the pastry sheets, starting with the filled edge. Arrange, seam side down, on a cookie sheet. Brush with melted butter and repeat, using the remaining filling and sheets of pastry.

Bake the rolls for 20–25 minutes, until golden, then serve.

These can be frozen in individual rolls and sliced as hors d'oeuvres or sliced into longer pieces and served as lunch. For a different presentation you can make individual phyllo triangles for hors d'oeuvres. Simply cut the phyllo into long strips, about $1\frac{1}{2}$ inches (.4 cm) wide, place one teaspoonful of the filling at the bottom of each strip and fold up at 45-degree angles to make a triangle shape.

Spring Rolls

Spring roll wrappers are available in most Asian markets; egg roll wrappers are in most super-markets. Spring rolls can be frozen for up to 3 months. Thaw them at room temperature for 1 hour, then pop them in an oven at 350°F (180°C) for 10–12 minutes.

Makes 12

1	whole chicken breast, split, skinned and deboned, then shredded	1
¼ cup	vegetable oil	50 mL
1 cup	diced celery	250 mL
1 cup	cleaned, diced mushrooms	250 mL
¼ cup	bean sprouts	50 mL
1 Tbsp.	soy sauce	15 mL
1 Tbsp.	cornstarch, dissolved in 2 Tbsp. (30 mL) cold water	15 mL
	spring roll or egg roll wrappers	
	vegetable oil for deep frying	
1 recipe	Lazy Plum Sauce (page 7)	1 recipe

Stir-fry chicken in oil in a skillet or wok over medium-high heat for 1 minute.

Add celery, mushrooms, bean sprouts and soy sauce to the chicken and stir-fry over medium-high heat for 30 seconds.

Add cornstarch dissolved in cold water to the pan. Stirring constantly, cook until the mixture thickens, about 5 minutes. Remove from heat and allow to cool.

Put ¼ cup (50 mL) of chicken mixture on each wrapper. Seal flaps with beaten egg or water.

Pour oil into a skillet to a depth of 1 inch (2.5 cm) and heat to medium-high—or heat oil in a deep fryer to a temperature of 375°F (190°C). Put rolls, a few at a time, in skillet or deep fryer, and fry for 3–5 minutes until golden brown, turning once. Remove with tongs and drain on paper towels.

Serve with Lazy Plum Sauce on the side.

Yakitori

Yakitori is delicious as an hors d'oeuvre but can also work as a main course. Serve with plain white rice and a cucumber salad, and dinner is ready.

Serves 4

6 Tbsp.	sherry	90 mL
¼ cup	soy sauce	50 mL
1 Tbsp.	sugar	15 mL
1	clove garlic, crushed	1
1 tsp.	minced ginger	5 mL
2	whole chicken breasts, split, skinned and deboned, then cut into ¾-inch (2-cm) pieces	2
2	bunches green onions, white part only, rinsed and cut into ¾-inch (2-cm) pieces	2

Make a marinade by combining sherry, soy sauce and sugar in a saucepan and bring to a boil. Reduce heat to low and simmer for about 10 minutes, until mixture has reduced by one-half. Remove from heat. Add the garlic and ginger, then transfer to a shallow baking dish and allow to cool.

Thread water-soaked wooden skewers with alternating pieces of chicken and green onions.

Marinate the skewers in refrigerator for 15 minutes, turning frequently.

Preheat oven to broil or grill.

Put skewers on a wire rack over a baking sheet and put the baking sheet in the oven, 4–5 inches (8–10 cm) from the element. Broil or grill for 2 minutes per side. Alternatively, cook skewers on an oiled barbecue, 4–5 inches (8–10 cm) from the heat, and cook for 2 minutes per side, basting often with the marinade. When chicken is cooked, coat with remaining sauce and serve.

Indonesian Chicken Satay

Be sure to make the Peanut Sauce ahead of time.

My guests have been known to refill their sauce bowls during dinner and put Peanut Sauce on whatever is being served, so you might want to make extra—it's delicious! Nam pla is available in Asian markets and some supermarkets.

Serves 4

2	whole chicken breasts, split, skinned and deboned, then cut into 1- x ½-inch (2.5- x 1-cm) strips	2
½ cup	finely chopped white onion	125 mL
3	cloves garlic, crushed	3
1 Tbsp.	minced ginger	15 mL
	juice of 1 lime	
1 Tbsp.	vegetable oil	15 mL
1 Tbsp.	nam pla (fish sauce)	15 mL
1 Tbsp.	brown sugar	15 mL
1 Tbsp.	finely chopped fresh cilantro	15 mL
1 recipe	Peanut Sauce (next page)	1 recipe

Make a marinade by combining onion, garlic, ginger, lime juice, oil, fish sauce and brown sugar in a bowl.

Marinate the chicken in the refrigerator for 1 hour, turning occasionally.

Preheat oven to broil or grill.

Thread water-soaked wooden skewers with chicken and put skewers on a wire rack over a baking sheet. Put the baking sheet in the oven, 4–5 inches (8–10 cm) from the element. Broil or grill for 2 minutes per side. Alternatively, cook skewers on an oiled barbecue, 4–5 inches (8–10 cm) from the heat, and cook for 2 minutes per side, basting often with marinade.

Serve with Peanut Sauce on the side.

Peanut Sauce

½ cup	crunchy peanut butter	125 mL
¾ cup	coconut cream	175 mL
1	white onion, finely chopped	1
1 Tbsp.	soy sauce	15 mL
1 Tbsp.	brown sugar	15 mL
2 tsp.	cayenne	10 mL
2	green onions, rinsed and chopped	2

Combine peanut butter, coconut cream, onion, soy sauce, brown sugar and cayenne in a saucepan and bring to a boil, stirring constantly, then remove from heat.

Add the green onions and mix together thoroughly, then chill in the refrigerator until ready to serve.

Vietnamese Fresh Salad Rolls

Make the rolls as close to serving time as possible, or the papers will dry out. To keep them fresh, soak paper towels with water. Squeeze out water and place over the rolls. Wrap tightly with plastic wrap.

Serves 8

8	pieces rice paper	8
6 oz.	rice vermicelli	170 g
8	romaine lettuce leaves, washed and patted dry	8
8 oz.	cooked chicken breast, cut into 1- x $\frac{1}{4}$-inch (3-cm) strips	200 g
8	1- x $\frac{1}{8}$-inch (3-cm) strips red pepper	8
8	green onions, washed and trimmed	8
1 recipe	Dipping Sauce (next page)	1 recipe

To prepare salad rolls, bring a pot of water to boiling. Add the rice vermicelli and remove pot from heat. Soak for 3–5 minutes, then pour into a colander. Rinse well with cold water and set aside.

Bring a fresh pot of water to boiling and remove from heat.

Immerse one sheet of rice paper in the water for 5 seconds, then remove and set aside.

Fold over the bottom third of the rice paper. Place one lettuce leaf on the portion of the rice paper that has been folded over. On top of the lettuce, put about $\frac{1}{8}$ of the vermicelli, then $\frac{1}{8}$ of the chicken, 1 strip of red pepper and 1 green onion with the green part extending past the rice paper.

Roll the folded bottom edge away from you, enclosing all the ingredients, to make a tight roll.

Repeat with the remaining ingredients.

Serve with Dipping Sauce.

Dipping Sauce

½ cup	hoisin sauce	125 mL
⅓ cup	prepared satay sauce	75 mL
	fresh cilantro leaves	
⅛ cup	roasted peanuts	25 mL

Mix hoisin sauce with satay sauce and thin with a little water to achieve a good consistency for dipping. Garnish with fresh cilantro and roasted peanuts.

Quesadillas

eel free to experiment with the filling. I sometimes add leftover grilled vegetables.

Serves 4

10	5-inch (12-cm) flour tortillas	10
1	egg, beaten	1
3 cups	grated cheddar cheese	750 mL
10 oz.	boneless chicken breast, grilled, cut into $\frac{1}{8}$- x $\frac{1}{4}$-inch (.3- x .5-cm) thick strips	300 g
2	red peppers, roasted, seeded, peeled and cut into $\frac{1}{4}$-inch (.5-cm) strips	2
$\frac{1}{4}$ cup	fresh cilantro leaves	50 mL
1	jalapeño pepper, seeded and chopped fine	1

Preheat oven to 350°F (180°C).

Brush 5 tortillas with beaten egg. Mix remaining ingredients together and spread equally over the 5 tortillas. Place a second tortilla on top of each of the prepared tortillas and press gently. Brush remaining egg on top and press around edges to seal.

Place tortillas on baking sheets for about 10 minutes, or until golden.

Let cool for 3 minutes, then cut into wedges. Serve with your favorite salsa.

Pizza with Wild Mushrooms and Grilled Chicken

This flavor combination is delectable, but if you don't like the taste of goat cheese, try using fontina cheese for a smoother taste.

Makes 1 12-in (30-cm) pizza

1 pkg.	dough mix for 12-inch (30-cm) pizza	1 pkg.
3–4 Tbsp.	butter	45–60 mL
2 Tbsp.	oil	30 mL
¼ lb.	wild mushrooms (chanterelles, shiitake or oyster), wiped clean and sliced	100 g
2	cloves garlic, crushed	2
2 Tbsp.	shallots, minced	30 mL
2	yellow peppers, cleaned, seeded and thinly sliced	2
¼ cup	sun-dried tomatoes, thinly sliced	50 mL
2	skinless, boneless, chicken breasts, grilled and cut into 1- x ¼-inch (2.5- x .5-cm) strips	2
3 oz.	goat cheese (chèvre)	75 g
3 oz.	mozzarella cheese	75 g
2 oz.	Parmesan cheese	50 g
1 Tbsp.	oil	15 mL

Prepare pizza dough according to instructions on package.

Preheat oven to 475°F (250°C).

Heat butter and oil in a skillet until sizzling. Sauté mushrooms, garlic and shallots for at least 5 minutes, until soft. Add yellow peppers and cook an additional 5 minutes. Add sun-dried tomatoes and cook 3 more minutes. Stir chicken into the vegetables and set aside.

Grate cheeses together and set aside.

Brush pizza crust with oil. Spread vegetable-chicken mixture over crust. Cover pizza evenly with grated cheese.

Bake for 18–20 minutes, until cheese is bubbling.

Asian Chicken in Phyllo Nests

To reduce stress when enter-taining, prepare the nests ahead. They can be frozen in a single layer in an airtight container for up to a month. Remove from freezer and recrisp in 350°F (175°C) oven for 3 minutes.

Makes 24

1¼ lbs.	boneless, skinless chicken breast, cooked and cut into ¼-inch (.5-cm) cubes	560 g
2 Tbsp.	soy sauce	30 mL
3 Tbsp.	rice wine vinegar	45 mL
¼ cup	peanut oil	50 mL
⅛ cup	vegetable oil	25 mL
14	sprigs parsley, chopped	14
4	green onions, thinly sliced	4
24	Phyllo Nests (next page)	24

Combine cooked chicken with soy sauce, rice wine vinegar, oils, parsley and green onions.

Spoon mixture evenly into prepared phyllo cups and serve warm.

Phyllo Nests

Makes 144

1	16-oz. (500-g) pkg. phyllo pastry, thawed	1
¾ cup	melted butter	175 mL

Preheat oven to 375°F (190°C).

Unwrap and unroll phyllo. Place one sheet on work surface. Cover remaining phyllo with dampened dish towel to keep moist.

Brush phyllo sheet lightly with butter. Top with a second sheet and brush with butter. Repeat with a third sheet. Cut lengthwise into 4 strips and crosswise into 6 strips to make 24 squares.

Press each square into a mini muffin or tart tin. Bake for 5 minutes, until golden. Remove from oven and place pan on a wire rack to cool.

Repeat with remaining phyllo.

Sun-dried Tomato and Chicken Bundles

These bundles are a wonderful combination of creamy cheeses, flaky pastry and flavorful sun-dried tomatoes.

Makes 24 bundles

1¼ lbs.	skinless, boneless chicken breast	565 g
	oil	
	salt and pepper to taste	
9 oz.	goat cheese	255 g
9 oz.	cream cheese	255 g
2 Tbsp.	sun-dried tomatoes (packed in oil), thinly sliced	30 mL
2 Tbsp.	finely chopped parsley	30 mL
1 Tbsp.	dried oregano leaves	15 mL
6	sheets phyllo, thawed	6
	olive oil for brushing	

Preheat oven to 350°F (180°C). Place chicken breasts on lightly oiled baking sheet. Season with salt and pepper and bake 15–20 minutes, until cooked through. Cool and slice into ¼-inch (.5-cm) pieces.

In a small bowl, combine chicken with the goat cheese, cream cheese, sun-dried tomatoes, parsley and oregano. Set aside until phyllo is prepared.

Preheat oven to 375°F (190°C).

To prepare phyllo, cut sheets in half to form 12- x 12-inch (30- x 30-cm) sheets. Place one sheet on your work surface. Keep remaining phyllo under a dampened dish towel to keep moist.

Lightly brush phyllo with melted butter. Top with a second sheet and brush with butter. Repeat with a third sheet. With a sharp knife cut phyllo into six 4-inch (10-cm) squares.

Place one heaping teaspoon (5 mL) of filling into center of each square. Bring together the four corners and edges of each square. Pinch around the filling and flare the top. Place on buttered baking sheet.

Repeat with remaining phyllo and filling. Bake 8–10 minutes, until golden.

These hors d'oeuvres can be made ahead and frozen. Once the bundles are prepared, freeze uncooked on trays. When they are frozen solid, they can be transferred to freezer bags. To prepare, bake straight from freezer at 375°F (190°C) for 10–12 minutes, until golden and heated through.

Soups and Sandwiches

S oup is an important part of many dining experiences. It can be a prelude to a meal or a meal in itself when served with a salad or sandwich. In this chapter, I have chosen clear soups and thick soups from a variety of cultures.

I like to keep chicken stock on hand in the freezer. With fresh chicken and vegetables added, it's a snap to pull together a delicious, nutritious meal!

Chicken Stock

Makes approximately 1¹⁄₂ quarts (1.5 L)

*A*lways keep this
stock on hand
in your freezer.

1	3-lb. (1.25-kg) boiler or stewing hen, thoroughly cleaned	1
1	white onion, quartered	1
1	carrot, halved	1
1	stalk celery, halved	1
1	leek, washed and chopped into 4-inch (10-cm) pieces	1
1	whole clove	1
1 tsp.	black peppercorns	5 mL

Place chicken in a large pot and cover with cold water. Bring to a boil, then skim off foam and other impurities.

Add remaining ingredients to pot and boil steadily for 1 hour. Remove chicken and vegetables from pot and strain the liquid through a colander lined with a cheesecloth into another pot. Let cool, then pour into an airtight plastic container, allowing space for expansion. Discard the vegetables and reserve the chicken for soups or salads. Chicken stock can be stored in the freezer for up to 6 months.

Mama Rozzie's Chicken Soup with Matzo Balls

This is my mother's Friday night special. She also makes it whenever I'm sick— it makes us both feel better.

Serves 4 to 6

2	3-lb. (1.25-kg) fryers or stewing hens, thoroughly cleaned	2
3	large white onions, quartered	3
8	carrots, halved	8
1	bunch celery, cut into 6-inch (15-cm) pieces	1
1 Tbsp.	finely chopped fresh parsley	15 mL
1 Tbsp.	finely chopped fresh dill	15 mL
	salt and freshly ground black pepper to taste	
	Matzo Balls (next page) or egg noodles	

Put chickens in a large pot and cover with cold water. Bring to a boil, and skim off any foam or other impurities. Reduce heat to low and simmer for 30 minutes, then skim again.

Add onions, carrots, celery, parsley, dill, salt and pepper and simmer over low heat for 2 hours, until chicken is tender.

Remove chickens and vegetables from pot and strain the liquid through a colander lined with a cheesecloth into another pot.

Discard the vegetables. Skin and debone the chickens, then dice and add chicken meat to soup, if desired.

Reheat stock to a simmer and add matzo balls or cooked egg noodles to hot soup just before serving.

Matzo Balls

Makes 10 to 12 balls

3	egg whites	3
	pinch of salt	
3	egg yolks, lightly beaten	3
½ cup	matzo meal	125 mL

Beat egg whites and salt in a bowl until soft peaks form.

Fold egg yolks into egg whites.

Stir matzo meal into the egg mixture and let sit in refrigerator for 2 hours or overnight. The mixture will go flat.

Fill a large pot with water and bring to a boil. Wet hands with cold water or vegetable oil and make small balls the size of walnuts out of the matzo ball mixture. Drop balls into the boiling water, reduce heat to low and simmer, covered, for 30–45 minutes. Remove from pot with a slotted spoon.

Mexican Chicken and Lime Soup

T his is my friend Deborah's *favorite soup. When she eats it, she thinks she's back on a Mexican holiday.*

Serves 4 to 6

½ cup	chopped white onion	125 mL
½	red pepper, seeded and julienned	½
1	green pepper, seeded and julienned	1
⅓ cup	chopped, canned green chilies	75 mL
2	cloves garlic, minced	2
¼ cup	vegetable oil	50 mL
4 cups	Chicken Stock (page 32)	1 L
½ tsp.	dried oregano leaves	2 mL
½ tsp.	dried marjoram leaves	2 mL
½ tsp.	dried thyme leaves	2 mL
	salt and freshly ground pepper to taste	
1	whole chicken breast, split, skinned and deboned, then cut into 1- x ¼-inch (2.5-cm x .6-cm) strips	1
2	firm, ripe tomatoes, julienned	2
3	green onions, rinsed and chopped	3
1 Tbsp.	finely chopped fresh cilantro	15 mL
	juice of 1 or 2 limes	
	tortilla chips	
2	limes, cut in wedges, or thinly sliced	2

Sauté onion, peppers, chilies and garlic in oil in a large pot over medium heat until onion is tender, about 5 minutes.

Add chicken stock, herbs, salt and pepper to the pot. Bring to a boil, reduce heat to low, cover and simmer for 20 minutes. Add chicken, tomatoes, green onions and cilantro and simmer for 10 more minutes.

Add lime juice and stir. Taste and add more juice, if desired.

Ladle into bowls. Add a few tortilla chips to each bowl. Serve with lime wedges on the side or float slices of lime on top.

Mulligatawny

Mulligatawny is a flavorful curry soup that originates in India. It is very easy to prepare if you have frozen chicken stock or use a good-quality prepared chicken stock from your grocer's freezer, and replace the spices with 3 Tbsp. (45 mL) curry powder.

Make a crisp salad, slice up some crusty breads or delicious Indian breads and voila! Dinner is ready.

Serves 6 to 8

1	white onion, quartered	1
2	carrots, peeled and quartered	2
2	stalks celery, quartered	2
1	leek, white part only, washed and cleaned, then cut into 1-inch (2.5-cm) pieces	1
1	tart apple, peeled, cored and quartered	1
2 Tbsp.	vegetable oil	30 mL
2 Tbsp.	unsalted butter	30 mL
3	sprigs fresh parsley, chopped	3
2	cloves garlic, chopped	2
1 tsp.	minced ginger	5 mL
2 tsp.	curry powder	10 mL
2 tsp.	ground cumin	10 mL
1 Tbsp.	ground turmeric	15 mL
1 tsp.	ground coriander	5 mL
	pinch mustard seed	
	pinch chili powder	
	pinch ground cloves	
	pinch ground mace	
4½ cups	Chicken Stock (page 32)	1 L + 125 mL
1	bay leaf	1
	salt and freshly ground pepper to taste	
2	whole chicken breasts, split, skinned and deboned, then cut into 1- x ¼-inch (2.5- x .6-cm) strips	2

½ cup	cooked rice	125 mL
1 Tbsp.	tomato paste	15 mL
1	firm, ripe tomato, peeled, seeded and finely chopped	1
3 Tbsp.	freshly squeezed lemon juice	45 mL
2 Tbsp.	finely chopped fresh cilantro	30 mL
2	limes, cut in wedges	2

Mince onion, carrots, celery, leek and apple in a food processor.

Sauté minced vegetables and apple in oil and butter in a large pot over medium heat for 5 minutes, until browned. Stir in herbs and spices.

Add chicken stock and bay leaf and bring to a boil. Reduce heat to low, cover and simmer for 25 minutes.

Season to taste with salt and pepper.

Add chicken, rice, tomato paste, tomato and lemon juice to the soup. Simmer for 5–10 minutes, stirring occasionally, until chicken is cooked through.

Ladle into bowls and garnish with chopped cilantro. Serve with lime wedges on the side.

Chinese Hot and Sour Soup

This soup is a delicious starter for an Asian meal. It's also lovely for lunch with some Spring Rolls on the side.

Serves 6 to 8

1	whole chicken breast, split, skinned, deboned, then cut into 1- x ¼-inch (2.5- x. 6-cm) strips	1
2 oz.	cooked ham, sliced very thinly, then julienned	50 g
8	dried Chinese black mushrooms, soaked in hot water for 30 minutes, then drained, stemmed and sliced	8
⅔ cup	slivered bamboo shoots	150 mL
6 cups	Chicken Stock (page 32)	1.5 L
1½ Tbsp.	soy sauce	20 mL
1½ cups	sliced tofu	375 mL
5 Tbsp.	red wine vinegar	75 mL
2 Tbsp.	cornstarch	30 mL
2	eggs, lightly beaten	2
1 tsp.	sesame oil	5 mL
	salt and freshly ground black pepper to taste	
2	green onions, rinsed and finely chopped	2

Put chicken, ham, mushrooms, bamboo shoots, chicken stock and soy sauce in a pot and bring to a boil. Reduce heat to low and simmer for 3 minutes.

Add tofu and red wine vinegar to the pot and bring to just under the boiling point. Dissolve cornstarch in 2 Tbsp. (30 mL) cold water and add to the pot.

Cook, stirring constantly, until soup thickens slightly, about 5 minutes. Slowly whisk eggs into soup in a steady stream to create threads of egg, then remove pot from heat. Add sesame oil and blend in. Season with salt and pepper. Ladle into bowls and garnish with chopped green onions.

Chicken and Coconut Soup

Galangal is also known as Laos root in Indonesia, or as Siamese ginger, because it is a member of the ginger family. However, it tastes different from ginger and adds flavor to Thai dishes. It can be frozen. Tamarind sauce is available in Asian markets and most supermarkets.

Serves 4 to 6

4 cups	water	1 L
½ cup	nam pla (fish sauce)	125 mL
28 oz.	coconut milk	796 mL
10	slices galangal (fresh, if possible)	10
6	shallots, minced very fine	6
2	cloves garlic, minced very fine	2
6 Tbsp.	tamarind sauce	90 mL
1	whole chicken breast, split, skinned and deboned, then cut into 1- x 1¼-inch (2.5- x .6-cm) strips	1
4 Tbsp.	chopped cilantro leaves	60 mL
4	red serrano chilies, crushed	4

In a large pot combine water, fish sauce, coconut milk, galangal, shallots, garlic and tamarind sauce. Bring to a boil over high heat.

Add the chicken to the pot, lower heat to medium and cook for about 10 minutes, until chicken is cooked thoroughly. Stir in the cilantro and chilies.

Chicken and Chinese Mushroom Soup

ilantro root adds a unique flavor to any chicken-based soup. Whenever I buy coriander, instead of throwing out the roots, I clean them very well and store them in the freezer in an airtight bag. When I make chicken soup from scratch, I throw some in whole, and remove them before serving.

Serves 4

4	cloves garlic	4
1 Tbsp.	cilantro root, washed well	15 mL
10	black peppercorns	10
2 Tbsp.	vegetable oil	30 mL
1	whole chicken breast, split, skinned and deboned, then cut into 1-x ¼-inch (2.5- x .6-cm) strips	1
5 cups	Chicken Stock (page 32)	1.2 L
8	dried Chinese mushrooms, soaked in hot water for 30 minutes, then drained, stemmed and thinly sliced	8
1 Tbsp.	fish sauce	15 mL
4	green onions, thinly sliced	4
4	sprigs cilantro	4
1 Tbsp.	fried garlic	15 mL

In a food processor, grind garlic cloves, cilantro root and peppercorns into a paste. This can also be done by hand with a mortar and pestle.

Add oil to a small saucepan and fry the paste over medium-low heat, stirring continuously for 1 minute. Do not burn. Add chicken breast and sauté until brown on all sides, about 3 to 4 minutes.

In a soup pot, mix together the chicken stock, mushrooms, fish sauce, and chicken. Bring to a boil, cover, reduce heat to low, and simmer for 15 minutes.

Add green onions and stir until softened. Ladle soup into bowls. Garnish with fresh cilantro and fried garlic.

Hot and Sour Chicken Soup with Lemon Grass

This soup is very popular in Thailand. Lemon grass is becoming more available. It is also available dried. If you cannot find any, substitute 2 tsp. (10 mL) grated lemon peel. The kaffir lime leaves and nam pla are available in Asian markets and some supermarkets.

When I make this for Ira I leave out the tomato.

Serves 4

2	slices galangal (see page 39)	2
3	stalks lemon grass, cut in 1-inch (2.5-cm) pieces	3
10	kaffir lime leaves, torn in half	10
4 cups	Chicken Stock (page 32)	
1	8-oz. (227-mL) can straw mushrooms, washed, strained and halved	1
1 cup	cooked chicken, sliced into 1- x ½-inch (2.5- x 1.2-cm) strips	
¾ lb.	king prawns, shelled and deveined	
¼ cup	lime juice	50 mL
3 Tbsp.	nam pla (fish sauce)	45 mL
3	spring onions, sliced very thin	3
2 Tbsp.	cilantro leaves	30 mL
4	serrano chilies, seeded and crushed	4
1	tomato, chopped into small dice	1

Place the lemon grass, galangal, 5 of the kaffir leaves and the chicken stock in a large pot. Bring to a boil and simmer gently for 5 minutes. The soup should already be fragrant. Strain soup and return to soup pot.

Add the mushrooms, chicken and prawns and heat until the prawns have turned pink, about 3–4 minutes.

Immediately stir in the lime juice, fish sauce, onions, cilantro, the rest of the lime leaves, serrano chilies and tomato. Stir 1 minute, then ladle into small bowls and serve.

Traditional Chicken Salad Sandwich

T he chicken filling can also be served on a bed of lettuce or on thin slices of Melba toast.

Serves 4 to 6

2	whole chicken breasts, split, skinned and deboned	2
½ cup	whipping cream	125 mL
2	tart apples, peeled, cored and julienned, then brushed with freshly squeezed lemon juice	2
¼–½ cup	sour cream	50–125 mL
¼–½ cup	Lemon Mayonnaise (next page)	50–125 mL
2 Tbsp.	finely chopped, seeded red pepper	30 mL
2 Tbsp.	toasted pine nuts	30 mL
2–3 tsp.	finely chopped fresh dill	7–15 mL
	salt and freshly ground black pepper to taste	
	fresh challah (egg bread)	
	butter to taste	
	lettuce leaves, rinsed	
	alfalfa sprouts	

Preheat oven to 350°F (180°C).

Put chicken in a 9-inch (22-cm) square baking dish.

Cover chicken with cream. Bake for 20–25 minutes, until chicken juices run clear (not pink) when pricked with a fork. Remove dish from oven and allow chicken to cool.

Shred into bite-size pieces and put in a bowl with the apples.

Combine sour cream, Lemon Mayonnaise, red pepper, pine nuts and dill in a bowl, then add to chicken and mix together.

Season with salt and pepper.

Serve on buttered fresh challah with lettuce underneath and alfalfa sprouts on top.

Lemon Mayonnaise

2	eggs	2
2 tsp.	Dijon mustard	10 mL
1 tsp.	salt	5 mL
2 cups	peanut oil	500 mL
4 Tbsp.	freshly squeezed lemon juice	60 mL
	pinch white pepper	

Combine eggs, mustard and salt in a food processor or blender.

With motor running, slowly add peanut oil in a thin, steady stream. Add lemon juice and blend. Season with pepper. Lemon Mayonnaise keeps up to 2 weeks in the refrigerator. It's nice to have on hand to impress your guests!

Chicken Club Sandwich

A Caesar salad turns this into a complete lunch. Some of your guests may only eat half a sandwich— they're large!

Serves 4 to 6

2	whole chicken breasts, split, skinned and deboned	2
2 Tbsp.	melted butter	30 mL
	salt and freshly ground black pepper to taste	
	juice of ½ lemon	
12	large slices black pumpernickel bread (3 slices per sandwich)	12
	butter to taste	
2	leaves romaine lettuce, rinsed and halved	2
4	slices tart apple, brushed with freshly squeezed lemon juice	4
	Lemon Mayonnaise to taste (page 43)	
6	slices bacon, halved and crisply cooked	6
1	ripe avocado, peeled, pitted and sliced, then brushed with freshly squeezed lemon juice	1

Preheat oven to 450°F (230°C).

Put chicken in a 9-inch (22-cm) square baking dish and brush with butter.

Season with salt and pepper, then sprinkle with lemon juice.

Cover dish with aluminum foil and bake for 8–10 minutes, until chicken is cooked through. Remove from oven, allow chicken to cool, and slice.

Spread butter evenly on 4 slices of bread, then put half a lettuce leaf on each slice of bread.

Divide chicken equally and place on top of lettuce leaves. Top chicken with one slice of apple. Spread Lemon Mayonnaise on apple slices.

Cover with 4 more slices of bread. Butter tops of bread slices. Divide bacon equally and place on top of second slices of bread. Put avocado slices on top of bacon. Spread Lemon Mayonnaise on avocado slices.

Cover with final 4 slices of bread, cut in half and serve.

Chicken Tacos

acos are always a fun-filled meal in our house because everyone helps prepare their own dinner. We always make extra guacamole for Joanna.

Prepared taco shells are available in most supermarkets if you need to save time.

Serves 4 to 6

2	whole chicken breasts, split, skinned and deboned	2
2 Tbsp.	melted butter	30 mL
	juice of ½ lemon	
1	white onion, finely chopped	1
1	large clove garlic, minced	1
2 Tbsp.	vegetable oil	30 mL
8	large, firm, ripe tomatoes, puréed	8
1	4-oz. (114-mL) can green chilies drained and diced	1
	salt and freshly ground black pepper to taste	
2 cups	grated cheddar cheese	500 mL
1 cup	shredded iceberg lettuce	250 mL
6	medium corn tortillas	6
	vegetable oil for deep frying	
1 recipe	Guacamole (next page)	1 recipe
1 recipe	Salsa (page 48)	1 recipe

Preheat oven to 450°F (230°C).

Put chicken in a 9-inch (22-cm) square baking dish and brush with butter. Sprinkle with lemon juice.

Cover dish with aluminum foil and bake for 8–10 minutes, until chicken is cooked thoroughly. Remove from oven. Allow chicken to cool, then dice, put in a large bowl and set aside.

Sauté onion and garlic in oil in a large skillet over medium heat for 5 minutes, then reduce heat to low.

Add tomatoes, green chilies, salt and pepper to skillet and simmer over low heat for 10 minutes, then add to chicken in bowl and mix together.

Put cheddar cheese and lettuce in separate bowls.

Fry corn tortillas, one at a time, in oil in a deep fryer at 375°F (190°C) for 45 seconds. Remove from deep fryer with tongs and fold tortillas in half. Return folded tortillas to deep fryer and fry for an additional 15 seconds, then remove from deep fryer with tongs and drain on paper towels.

Serve tortillas immediately, letting each person fill with a combination of chicken-vegetable filling, cheese and lettuce. Serve with Guacamole and Salsa on the side.

Guacamole

2	ripe avocados, peeled and pitted, reserving the pits	2
½	white onion, diced	½
2 Tbsp.	freshly squeezed lemon juice	30 mL
	dash of cayenne	

Mash avocados with a fork in a small bowl. Add remaining ingredients to avocados and mix together.

Put avocado pits in bowl to reduce discoloration, then cover and refrigerate until ready to serve. Remove pits from bowl before serving and discard.

Salsa

1	14-oz. (398-mL) can crushed tomatoes	1
1	firm, ripe tomato, finely chopped	1
¼ cup	tomato juice	50 mL
½	white onion, finely chopped	½
1–2	cloves garlic, minced	1–2
½	green pepper, seeded and finely chopped	½
1	jalapeño pepper, finely chopped	1
3 Tbsp.	finely chopped fresh parsley	50 mL
2–3 Tbsp.	freshly squeezed lemon juice	30–45 mL
1 tsp.	Worcestershire sauce	5 mL
1 tsp.	salt	5 mL
1 tsp.	freshly ground black pepper	5 mL

Combine all ingredients in a bowl. For an added treat, add some roasted corn.

Greek Chicken Sandwich

If you're watching calories, forget the pita and serve this as a salad instead.

Serves 4 to 6

2	whole chicken breasts, split, skinned and deboned	2
2 Tbsp.	melted butter	30 mL
	salt and freshly ground black pepper to taste	
	juice of ½ lemon	
4 Tbsp.	diced red onion	60 mL
4 Tbsp.	seeded, diced green pepper	60 mL
⅓	cucumber, diced	⅓
4 Tbsp.	pitted, sliced black olives	60 mL
¾ cup	mayonnaise	175 mL
2 Tbsp.	tomato juice	30 mL
1	clove garlic, crushed	1
	dash ground mace	
	salt and freshly ground black pepper to taste	
4–6	pita pocket breads	4–6

Preheat oven to 450°F (230°C).

Put chicken in a 9-inch (22-cm) square baking dish and brush with butter. Season with salt and pepper, and sprinkle with lemon juice.

Cover dish with aluminum foil and bake for 8–10 minutes, until chicken is cooked thoroughly, then remove dish from oven. Allow chicken to cool, dice and put in a bowl.

Add onions, green pepper, cucumber and olives to bowl. Stir in mayonnaise, tomato juice, garlic and mace. Season with salt and pepper.

Cut off tops of pita bread and open the pockets using your fingers. Fill with the chicken mixture.

Hot Chicken Parmesan Sandwiches

A dults and children alike delight in these sandwiches. Serve with Caesar salad and your favorite Chianti.

Serves 4 to 6

2	whole chicken breasts, split, skinned and deboned	2
5 Tbsp.	flour	75 mL
1 tsp.	dried oregano leaves	5 mL
½ tsp.	dried thyme leaves	2 mL
1 tsp.	salt	5 mL
1 tsp.	freshly ground black pepper	5 mL
1	large egg, lightly beaten	1
½ cup	corn flake crumbs	125 mL
½ cup	vegetable oil	125 mL
2 Tbsp.	unsalted butter	30 mL
4	large crusty Italian rolls, cut in half	4
4	large slices mozzarella cheese	4
1 recipe	Tomato Sauce (next page)	1 recipe
4 Tbsp.	freshly grated Parmesan cheese	60 mL

Pound chicken breasts between two pieces of waxed paper to a thickness of ¼ inch (.6 cm).

Mix flour, oregano, thyme, salt and pepper in a bowl, then dredge chicken in mixture.

Dip chicken in egg, shaking off the excess.

Roll chicken in corn flake crumbs until chicken is completely covered.

Sauté chicken in oil and butter in a skillet over medium heat for 6 minutes per side, then remove from skillet and drain on paper towels.

Preheat oven to broil or grill.

Put bottom half of rolls on a baking sheet. Place one chicken cutlet on each roll. Cover each cutlet with a slice of mozzarella cheese, then top cheese with Tomato Sauce.

Sprinkle with Parmesan cheese.

Put baking sheet in oven and broil or grill just until cheese has melted, about 2–3 minutes. Remove from oven, cover with top half of rolls, cut in half and serve.

Tomato Sauce

½ cup	tomato paste	125 mL
¼ cup	cold water	50 mL
1	clove garlic, minced	1
½ tsp.	sugar	2 mL
½ tsp.	dried oregano leaves	2 mL
½ tsp.	dried thyme leaves	2 mL
	salt and freshly ground black pepper to taste	

Combine all ingredients in a saucepan and cook over medium heat until sauce begins to bubble. Reduce heat to low and simmer, stirring occasionally, for 10 minutes.

Jerusalem Pita Pocket Sandwich

This is one of my favorite recipes. My friend Leah and I like to eat it with lots of tahini sauce and an eggplant salad on the side. Tahini paste is made from crushed sesame seeds.

Serves 4 to 6

2	whole chicken breasts, split, skinned and deboned	2
¼ cup	yogurt	50 mL
	juice of ½ lemon	
1 tsp.	ground cumin	5 mL
½ tsp.	ground coriander	2 mL
¼ tsp.	cayenne	1 mL
6	leaves romaine lettuce, rinsed and cut into bite-size pieces	6
2	firm, ripe tomatoes, seeded and diced	2
2	green onions, rinsed and chopped	2
⅓	cucumber, diced	⅓
¼ cup	toasted pine nuts	50 mL
4–6	pita pocket breads	4–6
1 recipe	Tahini Sauce (next page)	1 recipe

Make a marinade by combining yogurt, lemon juice, cumin, coriander and cayenne in a bowl. Marinate the chicken at room temperature for 2 hours.

Preheat oven to broil or grill.

Put chicken on a wire rack over a baking sheet. Broil or grill for 6 minutes per side, until chicken is cooked thoroughly. Remove baking sheet from oven, shred chicken into bite-size pieces and set aside in a bowl.

Combine lettuce, tomatoes, green onions, cucumber and pine nuts in bowl with chicken.

Slice the pita bread and open the pockets using your fingers. Fill with the chicken mixture.

Drizzle 1 Tbsp. (15 mL) Tahini Sauce over each pita and serve.

Tahini Sauce

¼ cup	tahini paste	50 mL
¼ cup	freshly squeezed lemon juice	50 mL
2	cloves garlic, chopped	2
	dash of salt	
	dash of cayenne	
½ cup	cold water	125 mL

Combine all ingredients except water in a food processor or a blender until smooth. Scrape sides, if necessary.

With motor running, slowly add water in a thin, steady stream until thoroughly blended.

Grilled Chicken and Mango Chapati Roll-ups

Serve on baby spinach with toasted cashews, and chapatis on the side. For an equally delicious combination, try papaya instead of mango. For a change of flavor, substitute a spicy peanut sauce for the Mango Dressing.

Serves 6

6	chapatis or rotis	6
4 cups	cooked basmati rice, warm	1 L
2 cups	grilled boneless breast of chicken	500 mL
2	sweet mangos, peeled, sliced and julienned	2
1 cup	grilled red pepper	250 mL
2	green onions, sliced very thin	2
¾–1 cup	Mango Dressing (next page)	175–250 mL

Place ⅔ cup (150 mL) basmati rice along the bottom of each chapati, leaving 2 inches (5 cm) of chapati on each side to be folded over.

For each chapati, top rice with ⅙ of the chicken, mango, red pepper and green onion.

Pour 2–3 Tbsp. (30–45 mL) Mango Dressing on top of each chapati. Fold the sides of each chapati toward the center, then roll up.

Cut roll-ups in half and serve with a green salad.

Mango Dressing

¼ cup	freshly squeezed lemon juice	50 mL
2 Tbsp.	red wine vinegar	30 mL
4 Tbsp.	sweet mango chutney	60 mL
2 Tbsp.	curry powder	30 mL
½ tsp.	salt	2 mL
½ tsp.	sugar	2 mL
¾ cup	light vegetable oil	175 mL

Combine all ingredients except oil in a food processor or blender, fitted with a metal blade. Mix on high speed for 3 minutes.

With motor running, add oil in a slow, steady stream. This sauce will keep in the refrigerator for 2 weeks.

Grilled Chicken Sandwich with Chèvre, Roasted Peppers and Arugula

erve with a salad of mixed baby greens with balsamic dressing.

Serves 4

2	whole chicken breasts, split, skinned, and deboned	2
3 Tbsp.	olive oil	45 mL
	salt and freshly ground black pepper	
4	fresh sandwich-sized rolls (e.g. kaisers), halved	4
1 cup	arugula	250 mL
1 Tbsp.	basil	15 mL
2	roasted red peppers (see below)	2
¾–1 cup	chèvre (goat cheese)	175–250 mL

Preheat oven to broil or grill.

In a small bowl, rub chicken with olive oil, salt and pepper.

Place chicken on a baking sheet and broil 5 inches (12 cm) from grill for 6 minutes per side, until cooked. Cool and slice into strips along diagonal. Divide chicken among the bottom halves of the buns. Top with arugula, basil and red peppers.

Spread top halves of buns with chèvre. Close the sandwiches and press together firmly. Cut in half and serve.

ROASTING RED PEPPERS:

To roast red pepper, place on cookie sheet 5–6 inches (12–15 cm) from preheated broiler. When one side turns puffy and black, turn with tongs until pepper is totally blackened. Put in bowl and cover with plastic wrap until cool. Remove blackened skin, seeds, ribs, and stem and cut into strips. They can be stored in olive oil for 1 week in the refrigerator or frozen between layers of waxed paper.

Grilled Chicken Sandwich with Peppers and Olivada

If you like olives, you'll love this sandwich.

Olive buns are found in specialty bread stores. If you cannot find them, use any delicious crusty bread.

Serves 4

2	whole chicken breasts, split, skinned and deboned	2
2 Tbsp.	olive oil	30 mL
	salt and freshly ground black pepper	
4	olive buns	4
2	red peppers, roasted, peeled, seeded and sliced thin (see page 56)	2
12	fresh basil leaves	12
¾ cup	baby spinach greens	175 mL
¾ cup	Olivada (next page)	175 mL

Preheat oven to broil or grill.

In a small bowl rub chicken with oil, salt and pepper. Place chicken on a baking sheet and broil 4–5 inches (10–12 cm) from grill for 6 minutes per side, until cooked thoroughly. Remove from oven. Cool slightly and slice into strips along the diagonal.

Divide chicken among the bottom halves of the buns. Top with roasted red peppers, basil and spinach.

Spread top halves of buns with Olivada. Close the sandwiches and press together firmly. Cut in half and serve.

If you want a special treat, try Red Pepper Coulis (next page).

Olivada

3 cups	black olives, pitted	700 mL
2 Tbsp.	olive oil	30 mL
	freshly ground black pepper to taste	

Place the olives in the bowl of a food processor fitted with a metal blade. Process until puréed. With motor running, add olive oil slowly until a smooth paste is formed. Season with freshly ground pepper.

Red Pepper Coulis

¼ cup	olive oil	50 mL
6	cloves garlic, minced	6
3	sweet red peppers, seeded, sliced thin	3
1 Tbsp.	balsamic vinegar	15 mL
1 tsp.	sugar	5 mL
	salt and pepper to taste	
2 Tbsp.	sun-dried tomato pesto	30 mL
1/4 cup	basil leaves, chopped	50 mL

Heat oil in skillet and add garlic. Sauté for 30 seconds, add red peppers, and continue cooking over medium heat for 15 minutes. Stir in vinegar, sugar, salt and pepper. Continue cooking for 20 minutes. Add tomato pesto and basil. Stir and set aside to cool.

Salads

A salad is a salad is a salad—except in this chapter, where a salad can be an entire meal! Most of the recipes in this chapter are great in small portions with a meal, or perfect as one-dish luncheons, served with interesting breads on the side.

Salads can be taken to the beach or the park in the afternoon, or they look great as part of a spread at a buffet dinner party. If taking chicken salad to the beach or park, though, make sure that it is packed in a cooler after being thoroughly chilled.

The recipes in this chapter use various methods of cooking chicken, but you can use leftover chicken from meals or stock-making. Remember, a salad is a great way to use leftover chicken!

Tarragon Chicken Salad with Pasta Shells

This is a light, lovely salad— perfect for a summer's day!

Serves 4 to 6

¼ lb.	fresh pasta shells or 1 cup (250 mL) dried pasta shells	125 g
2	whole chicken breasts, split, skinned and deboned, then cut into bite-size pieces	2
2 Tbsp.	vegetable oil	30 mL
2 cups	seeded, julienned red pepper	500 mL
2 cups	seeded, julienned green pepper	500 mL
¼ lb.	snow peas, lightly steamed	125 g
1	bunch green onions, rinsed and chopped	1
1 recipe	Tarragon Dressing (next page)	1 recipe

Cook pasta shells al dente in a pot of boiling salted water: 3–5 minutes for fresh pasta; 5–7 minutes for dried pasta. Drain and rinse well with cold water. Drain well, then put in a large bowl.

Sauté chicken in oil in a skillet over medium heat for 2–3 minutes until chicken is cooked through and color becomes opaque. Remove from skillet with a slotted spoon and add to bowl with pasta.

Add peppers, snow peas and green onions to bowl and mix together.

Pour Tarragon Dressing over salad, toss and serve.

Tarragon Dressing

½ cup	safflower oil	125 mL
¼ cup	freshly squeezed lemon juice	50 mL
4	cloves garlic, crushed	4
1 tsp.	minced ginger	5 mL
1 Tbsp.	dried tarragon leaves	15 mL
	salt and freshly ground black pepper to taste	

Whisk all the ingredients in a bowl. Use as much or as little as you would like, storing the rest in the refrigerator for up to a week.

Chicken Primavera Salad

Serve as a picnic lunch or an evening meal when you want something light on a hot day! I recommend using an aged balsamic vinegar when preparing salad dressings. Although they are more expensive per bottle, you use very little and you can really taste the difference.

Serves 4 to 6

2	whole chicken breasts, split, skinned and deboned, then cut into bite-size pieces	2
2 tsp.	dried basil leaves	10 mL
2 tsp.	paprika	10 mL
2 tsp.	garlic powder	10 mL
2 tsp.	cayenne	10 mL
2 tsp.	salt	10 mL
2 tsp.	white pepper	10 mL
1	egg, lightly beaten	1
½ cup	milk	125 mL
¾ cup	flour	175 mL
3	cloves garlic, minced	3
½ cup	finely chopped fresh parsley	125 mL
½ cup	vegetable oil	125 mL
½ cup	unsalted butter	125 mL
2–3	carrots, peeled and julienned	2–3
½ cup	seeded, julienned red pepper	125 mL
½ cup	seeded, julienned green pepper	125 mL
½ cup	seeded, julienned yellow pepper	125 mL
½ cup	snow peas, cut diagonally	125 mL
1 cup	shredded red cabbage	250 mL
1 recipe	Green Onion Mayonnaise (next page)	1 recipe

In a bowl, combine basil, paprika, garlic powder, cayenne, salt and pepper. Toss the chicken with half the seasoning mix in a bowl or paper bag.

Blend the egg and milk together in a bowl, then add chicken. Allow it to soak for 1 minute, then drain.

Mix flour and remaining seasoning mix together in a bowl. Dredge chicken in mixture.

Sauté garlic and parsley in oil and butter in a skillet over medium heat for 1 minute.

Add chicken, a few pieces at a time, to skillet and sauté over medium heat for 3–4 minutes until cooked through and golden colored. Remove from skillet with a slotted spoon, drain on paper towels and set aside to cool.

Mix carrots, peppers, snow peas and red cabbage in a large glass bowl.

Add chicken and dressing to the bowl. Toss together.

Green Onion Mayonnaise

1	egg	1
1½ Tbsp.	Dijon mustard	20 mL
1 cup	vegetable oil	250 mL
1 Tbsp.	balsamic vinegar	15 mL
	salt and freshly ground black pepper to taste	
4	green onions, rinsed and chopped	4

Blend the egg and mustard in a food processor or blender.

With motor running, slowly add the oil in a thin, steady stream.

Add the balsamic vinegar, salt and pepper and blend in.

Mix in green onions by hand. Use as much or as little dressing as you like, storing the rest in the refrigerator for up to 2 weeks.

Pesto Pasta Chicken Salad

This is great for a party! For a colorful presentation try this salad with a variety of different colored rotini.

Serves 6 to 8

½ lb.	fresh rotini pasta or 1¾ cups (425 mL) dried rotini	250 g
3	whole chicken breasts, split, skinned and deboned, then cut into bite-size pieces	3
3 Tbsp.	vegetable oil	45 mL
1	6½-oz. (184-mL) jar artichoke hearts, drained and quartered	1
½ cup	finely chopped red onion	125 mL
4	green onions, rinsed and chopped	4
1 cup	peeled, julienned carrots	250 mL
⅔ cup	chopped celery	150 mL
½ cup	seeded, julienned red pepper	125 mL
½ cup	seeded, julienned green pepper	125 mL
½ cup	shredded red cabbage	125 mL
¾ cup	julienned zucchini, peel on	175 mL
6	radishes, rinsed and thinly sliced	6
⅔ cup	pitted, sliced black olives	150 mL
1 recipe	Lemon Pesto Dressing (next page)	1 recipe
2 Tbsp.	toasted pine nuts	30 mL

Cook rotini al dente in a pot of boiling salted water: for 3–5 minutes for fresh pasta; 5–7 minutes for dried pasta. Drain and rinse well with cold water. Drain well, then put in a large bowl.

Sauté chicken in oil in a skillet over medium heat for 2–3 minutes until chicken is cooked through and color becomes opaque. Remove from skillet with a slotted spoon and add to bowl with pasta.

Add the remaining ingredients except the Lemon Pesto Dressing and pine nuts to the bowl and toss together.

Top with Lemon Pesto Dressing and toss lightly. Garnish with toasted pine nuts and serve.

Lemon Pesto Dressing

⅓ cup	red wine vinegar	75 mL
2 Tbsp.	freshly squeezed lemon juice	30 mL
2 Tbsp.	Pesto Sauce (below)	30 mL
2	cloves garlic, chopped	2
½ cup	stemmed fresh parsley	125 mL
	salt and freshly ground pepper to taste	
1¼ cups	olive oil	300 mL

Combine all the ingredients except the olive oil in a food processor or blender.

With motor running, slowly add the olive oil in a thin, steady stream. Use as much or as little dressing as you would like, storing the rest in the refrigerator for up to a week.

Pesto Sauce

1 cup	fresh basil leaves	250 mL
¼ cup	olive oil	50 mL
1	clove garlic, chopped	1
1½ Tbsp.	toasted pine nuts	20 mL
1 Tbsp.	freshly grated Parmesan cheese	15 mL
1 tsp.	salt	5 mL

Purée all the ingredients in a food processor or blender until smooth. Store in an airtight container in the freezer.

Pesto Sauce keeps up to 6 months in your freezer, so you can prepare ahead to save time when you're entertaining. If you're feeling particularly lazy or rushed . . . as I often am . . . there are now several excellent pesto sauces available fresh in local grocery stores. They are usually found on the refrigerated shelf with fresh pastas.

Mexican Green Chili Salad

This salad is spicy and crunchy! Be sure to make the dressing the day before!

Serves 6

2	whole chicken breasts, split, skinned and deboned	2
2 Tbsp.	melted butter	30 mL
	juice of ½ lemon	
½ cup	rinsed, finely chopped green onions	125 mL
2	firm, ripe tomatoes, seeded and chopped	2
1	green pepper, seeded and chopped	1
½ cup	seeded, chopped green chilies	125 mL
1	14-oz. (398-mL) can baby corn, drained and sliced in half lengthwise	1
1 cup	grated cheddar cheese	250 mL
1	head iceberg lettuce, cored and shredded	1
1 recipe	Tangy Herb Dressing (next page)	1 recipe
2 Tbsp.	pitted, sliced black olives	30 mL
1 cup	toasted pine nuts	125 mL

Preheat oven to 450°F (230°C).

Put chicken in a 9-inch (22-cm) square baking dish and brush with butter. Sprinkle with lemon juice.

Cover dish with aluminum foil and bake for 8–10 minutes, until chicken is cooked thoroughly. Remove from oven, allow chicken to cool, then dice and put in a large bowl.

Add vegetables, cheese and lettuce to chicken in bowl and mix together.

Top with dressing and toss lightly. Garnish with sliced olives and pine nuts. Refrigerate for at least 15 minutes before serving.

Tangy Herb Dressing

½ cup	vegetable oil	125 mL
2 Tbsp.	cider vinegar	30 mL
1 Tbsp.	freshly squeezed lemon juice	15 mL
1	clove garlic, crushed	1
½ tsp.	dried thyme leaves	2 mL
½ tsp.	dried oregano leaves	2 mL
½ tsp.	dried marjoram leaves	2 mL
	salt and freshly ground pepper to taste	

Combine all the ingredients in a jar with a tightly fitting lid. Shake thoroughly, then chill in the refrigerator overnight.

Sesame-Soy Chicken Salad with Crunchy Vegetables

I love this salad! It's been a family favorite for almost two decades and continues to delight friends and family alike.

Serves 4 to 6

2	whole chicken breasts, split, skinned and deboned, then cut into bite-size pieces	2
2 Tbsp.	vegetable oil	30 mL
1 cup	cauliflower florets	250 mL
1 cup	broccoli florets	250 mL
4	carrots, peeled and julienned	4
1	zucchini, julienned, peel on	1
½ cup	snow peas	125 mL
½ cup	cleaned, sliced mushrooms	125 mL
½ cup	shredded red cabbage	125 mL
1 recipe	Ginger Sesame Dressing (next page)	1 recipe
2 Tbsp.	toasted sesame seeds	30 mL

Sauté chicken in oil in a skillet over medium heat for 2–3 minutes until chicken is cooked and color becomes opaque. Remove from skillet with a slotted spoon and set aside.

Steam cauliflower and broccoli for 6 minutes over boiling water, then rinse with cold water, drain well and set aside.

Steam carrots for 4–5 minutes over boiling water, then rinse with cold water, drain well and set aside.

Steam zucchini for 2–3 minutes over boiling water, then rinse with cold water, drain well and set aside.

Steam snow peas for 1 minute over boiling water, then rinse with cold water, drain well and set aside.

Put mushrooms and cabbage in a large glass bowl. Add chicken and steamed vegetables and mix together.

Top with Ginger Sesame Dressing and toss lightly. Garnish with toasted sesame seeds (see page 7).

Ginger Sesame Dressing

4 Tbsp.	red wine vinegar	60 mL
2 Tbsp.	soy sauce	30 mL
1	clove garlic, chopped	1
2 tsp.	minced ginger	10 mL
1 tsp.	sugar	5 mL
¾ cup	vegetable oil	175 mL
3	drops sesame oil	3
2 Tbsp.	toasted sesame seeds	30 mL

Combine the red wine vinegar, soy sauce, garlic, ginger and sugar in a food processor or blender.

With motor running, slowly add oils in a thin, steady stream.

Stir in the sesame seeds by hand. Use as much or as little as you like, storing the rest in the refrigerator.

Szechuan Chicken Salad

Make the peanut sauce before preparing the salad.

This salad has a very dramatic presentation. It is lovely as a one-dish lunch for a small group or as a focal point on a large buffet spread.

Serves 4 to 6

1	green onion, rinsed and cut into 1-inch (2.5-cm) pieces	1
1 tsp.	minced ginger	5 mL
3	whole chicken breasts, split, skinned and deboned	3
1	head butter lettuce, broken into leaves, washed and dried	1
1	English cucumber, thinly sliced	1
½	4-oz. (113-g) pkg. mung bean noodles	½
8	large mushrooms, cleaned and thinly sliced	8
½ cup	julienned snow peas	125 mL
¼	large red cabbage, finely shredded	¼
8	large radishes, rinsed and thinly sliced	8
1 recipe	Spicy Peanut Sauce (next page)	1 recipe
2	green onions, rinsed and chopped	2
3 Tbsp.	toasted crushed peanuts (page 7)	45 mL

Put green onion and ginger in a pot with enough cold water to cover the chicken and bring to a boil.

Add chicken to the pot, reduce heat to low and simmer for 5 minutes. Cover pot and remove from heat. Let chicken steep for 2 hours. Drain pot, reserving stock for other uses. Allow chicken to cool, then shred into bite-size pieces and set aside.

Line a large shallow serving platter with lettuce leaves. Form a ring of overlapping layers of cucumber around outer edge of dish.

Put noodles in a bowl and cover with hot water. Soak until they are silky, drain well, then cut noodles in half. Form an inner ring of noodles, overlapping the cucumber slices.

Toss mushrooms, snow peas, cabbage and radishes in a bowl, then mound them in the middle of the serving dish.

Spoon chicken on top of the mound of vegetables. Pour Spicy Peanut Sauce over chicken.

Garnish with chopped green onions and toasted crushed peanuts. Toss at table and serve.

Spicy Peanut Sauce

½ cup	crunchy peanut butter	125 mL
½ cup	sugar	125 mL
7 Tbsp.	soy sauce	105 mL
1 Tbsp.	hot chili sauce	15 mL
1 tsp.	sherry	5 mL
3–4	cloves garlic, chopped	3–4
1 Tbsp.	finely chopped fresh cilantro	15 mL

Combine all the ingredients in a food processor or blender until smooth. Store in refrigerator, but serve at room temperature. Use as much or as little as you like, storing the rest in the refrigerator.

Indochina Vermicelli Salad

on't let the number of ingredients fool you into thinking this is a difficult dish to make. Both the dressing and the chicken can be prepared the day before, the vegetables can be sliced and diced handily with a sharp knife or mandoline. It makes a terrific party salad!

Serves 8 to 10

¾ lb.	dried vermicelli pasta	350 g
1	green onion, rinsed and cut into 1-inch (2.5-cm) pieces	1
1 tsp.	minced ginger	5 mL
4	whole chicken breasts, split, skinned and deboned	4
1 cup	bok choy, chopped	250 mL
1 cup	sui choy, chopped	250 mL
1½ cups	trimmed, chopped broccoli florets	375 mL
1 cup	rinsed, chopped green onions	250 mL
¾ lb.	bean sprouts	350 g
2	bunches radishes, rinsed and very thinly sliced	2
4 Tbsp.	coarsely chopped toasted cashews	60 mL
1 recipe	Tangy Peanut Dressing (next page)	1 recipe

Cook vermicelli al dente in a pot of boiling salted water for 5–7 minutes. Drain and rinse well with cold water. Drain well, then put in a large bowl.

Put green onion and ginger in a pot with enough cold water to cover the chicken and bring to a boil.

Add chicken to the pot, reduce heat to low and simmer for 5 minutes. Cover pot and remove from heat. Let chicken steep for 2 hours. Drain pot, reserving stock for other uses. Allow chicken to cool, then shred into bite-size pieces and add to bowl with pasta.

Add vegetables and cashews to bowl and mix together.

Top with Tangy Peanut Dressing and toss lightly.

Tangy Peanut Dressing

1¾ cups	safflower oil	425 mL
¼ cup	red wine vinegar	50 mL
2 Tbsp.	freshly squeezed lemon juice	30 mL
2 Tbsp.	soy sauce	30 mL
1	clove garlic, chopped	1
½ tsp.	cayenne	2 mL
	dash Worcestershire sauce	
	salt and freshly ground black pepper to taste	
⅔ cup	natural peanut butter	150 mL

Blend everything except the peanut butter in a food processor or blender.

Blend in the peanut butter by hand. Use as much or as little of the dressing as you like, storing the rest in the refrigerator.

Curried Chicken Salad

This salad looks wonderful on a bed of lettuce or, for special lunches, serve in cantaloupe halves.

Serves 4 to 6

2	whole chicken breasts, split, skinned and deboned, then cut into bite-size pieces	2
2 Tbsp.	vegetable oil	30 mL
¼ cup	finely chopped red onion	50 mL
1 cup	chopped celery	250 mL
¾ cup	cleaned, sliced mushrooms	175 mL
½ cup	seeded, coarsely chopped red pepper	125 mL
½ cup	seeded, coarsely chopped green pepper	125 mL
½ cup	snow peas, lightly steamed	125 mL
½ cup	halved seedless red grapes	125 mL
½ cup	halved seedless green grapes	125 mL
½ cup	toasted sliced almonds	50 mL
1 recipe	Creamy Curried Dressing (next page)	1 recipe

Sauté chicken in oil in a skillet over medium heat for 2–3 minutes until chicken is cooked and color becomes opaque. Remove from skillet with a slotted spoon and put in a large bowl.

Add the remaining ingredients to the chicken and mix together.

Top with dressing and toss lightly.

Creamy Curried Dressing

⅓ cup	whipped cream cheese	75 mL
⅓ cup	yogurt	75 mL
½ cup	mayonnaise	125 mL
1 Tbsp.	liquid honey	15 mL
1½ tsp.	curry powder	7 mL
3	dashes hot pepper sauce	3
	freshly ground black pepper to taste	

Combine all the ingredients in a food processor or blender. Use as much or as little as you like, storing the rest in the refrigerator.

Spa Asian Chicken Salad

*I serve this salad
on its own for a
delicious low-
calorie, low-fat
lunch. Add some
shrimp chips on the
side, and lunch is
ready.*

Serves 6

2	whole chicken breasts, split, skinned and deboned	2
3 Tbsp.	soy sauce	45 mL
2 Tbsp.	mirin (rice wine)	30 mL
1 tsp.	sesame oil	5 mL
2	heads Boston leaf lettuce, separated, or iceberg lettuce, shredded	2
3	carrots, shredded	3
2	red peppers, seeded and sliced very thin	2
4	green onions, sliced thin	4
2 cups	bean sprouts	500 mL
1 recipe	Garlicky Peanut Dressing (next page)	1 recipe
¾ cup	cilantro leaves	175 mL
1	orange, peeled, sliced thin	1
½ cup	seedless grapes, halved	125 mL

In a bowl, combine soy sauce, mirin, sesame oil and chicken
breasts. Cover and refrigerate for 2 hours.

Preheat barbecue or oven broiler. Put chicken on oiled
barbecue 5–6 inches (12–15 cm) from heat, or place on a
baking sheet and broil 5 inches (12 cm) from element. Cook
6 minutes on each side, until chicken is cooked thoroughly.

Remove from grill and cool slightly. Cut into long, thin strips
and set aside.

Arrange lettuce leaves or shredded lettuce on 6 plates.

Mix together carrots, red peppers, green onions and bean sprouts and divide equally among the lettuce leaves.

Distribute sliced chicken over each plate. Pour Garlicky Peanut Dressing generously over each plate and garnish with orange slices, grapes and cilantro.

Garlicky Peanut Dressing

4	cloves garlic, minced	4
⅓ cup	rice vinegar	75 mL
½ cup	smooth peanut butter	125 mL
1 Tbsp.	soy sauce	15 mL
1 tsp.	sugar	5 mL
1 tsp.	hot Asian chili sauce	5 mL
1 tsp.	sesame oil	5 mL
⅔ cup	water	150 mL

Combine all the ingredients, except water, in a food processor or blender. With motor running, slowly add the water in a slow and steady stream. Use as much or as little dressing as you like, storing the rest in the refrigerator for up to 2 weeks.

This dressing is very thin. Do not be alarmed. It is very rich in flavor.

Laotian Chicken Salad

This is so fresh-tasting on a hot summer day. If you cannot find green mango, you can always substitute tart green apple.

Serves 4 to 6

2	whole chicken breasts, split, skinned and deboned	2
1 Tbsp.	soy sauce	15 mL
1 tsp.	lime juice	5 mL
1 tsp.	Asian chili sauce	5 mL
1	head Boston lettuce, torn into bite-size pieces	1
1	green mango, peeled and cut into thin slivers	1
½	long English cucumber, julienned	½
1	red pepper, thinly sliced	1
½ cup	seedless green grapes, halved	125 mL
¼	red onion, julienned	¼
4	sprigs cilantro	4
1 recipe	Cilantro Lime Dressing (next page)	1 recipe

Make a marinade by combining soy sauce, lime juice and chili sauce in a small bowl.

Add chicken to bowl and coat all over with the sauce. Cover and marinate for 1 hour in the refrigerator.

Preheat barbecue or oven broiler.

Put chicken on an oiled barbecue 5–6 inches (12–15 cm) from heat, or place on a baking sheet and broil, 5 inches (12 cm) from element.

Cook 6 minutes on each side, until chicken is cooked thoroughly. Remove from grill and cool. Cut into strips and place in a large bowl.

Add all remaining ingredients except coriander sprigs to bowl.
Toss with Cilantro Lime Dressing. Garnish with cilantro sprigs.

Cilantro Lime Dressing

5 Tbsp.	sugar	75 mL
½ cup	water	125 mL
⅓ cup	lime juice	75 mL
1 Tbsp.	nam pla (fish sauce)	15 mL
1 Tbsp.	cilantro leaves	15 mL
1 tsp.	chili garlic sauce	5 mL

Combine all ingredients in a food processor or
blender until smooth.

Gado Gado Chicken Salad

Make the Gado Gado Sauce ahead.

This is a delicious Indonesian dish. Sambal badjak is a hot chili relish made of red chilies, sugar, oil, shallots and spices. Don't confuse it with sambal oeleck, which has only chilies, water, sugar and salt.

Serves 6 to 8

4	whole chicken breasts, split, skinned and deboned	4
4 Tbsp.	soy sauce	60 mL
2 Tbsp.	lime juice	30 mL
2 Tbsp.	vegetable oil	30 mL
2 tsp.	sesame oil	10 mL
1	1-lb. (454-g) pkg. thin vermicelli noodles, cooked according to package directions	1
3	sweet mangos, peeled and cut into thin slivers	3
6	green onions, sliced thin	6
2	red peppers, julienned	2
5 Tbsp.	cilantro leaves	75 mL
⅓ cup	crushed toasted peanuts	75 mL
6	sprigs cilantro	6
1 recipe	Gado Gado Sauce (next page)	1 recipe

Mix soy sauce, lime juice, vegetable oil and sesame oil together in a small bowl. Add chicken and coat all over with sauce. Cover and marinate for 1 hour in refrigerator.

Preheat barbecue or oven broiler.

Place chicken an on oiled barbecue 5–6 inches (12–15 cm) from heat, or place on a baking sheet and broil 5 inches (12 cm) from element. Cook for 6 minutes on each side, until chicken is cooked thoroughly. Remove from grill and cool. Slice thinly on the diagonal and set aside.

Arrange mangos around the edges of a large circular platter.

Place cooled vermicelli noodles on top of mangos, leaving the outer corners of mangos visible.

In a bowl, toss green onions, red peppers, cilantro and chicken slices with Gado Gado Sauce and arrange over chilled noodles.

Garnish with peanuts and cilantro sprigs.

Gado Gado Sauce

1 Tbsp.	vegetable oil	15 mL
½	white onion, diced	½
1	clove garlic, diced	1
1½ Tbsp.	ginger, grated	20 mL
½ tsp.	sambal badjak	2 mL
2 tsp.	soy sauce	10 mL
2 tsp.	brown sugar	10 mL
1 tsp.	honey	5 mL
1 Tbsp.	lemon juice	15 mL
½ cup	peanut butter	125 mL
1 cup	coconut milk	250 mL

Heat oil in saucepan over medium-high heat. Add onion, garlic, ginger and sambal badjak and sauté until onion becomes transparent.

Add the remaining ingredients except coconut milk in the order in which they are listed, stirring constantly over medium heat. Reduce heat to low and simmer for 5 minutes, stirring constantly.

Blend in coconut milk, remove from heat and allow to cool before serving.

Fusion Chicken Salad with Chèvre and Roasted Pecans

Be sure to make extra roasted pecans. They are so tasty it's the only way to ensure you'll have enough for the salad.

Serves 6

3	whole chicken breasts, split, skinned and deboned	3
3 Tbsp.	mirin (rice wine)	45 mL
1	clove garlic, minced	1
2 tsp.	black pepper	10 mL
1 Tbsp.	vegetable oil	15 mL
¾ cup	chèvre (goat cheese)	175 mL
6 cups	mixed salad greens	1.5 L
1 cup	roasted pecans, broken into pieces (next page)	250 mL
6	sprigs cilantro	6
1 recipe	Ginger Cilantro Dressing (next page)	1 recipe

Mix together mirin, garlic, pepper and vegetable oil in a small bowl. Add chicken breasts, turning with a fork until each piece is completely coated with mixture. Cover bowl and marinate for 1 hour in the refrigerator.

Preheat oven broiler.

Place chicken on a baking sheet and broil 4–5 inches (10–12 cm) from element. Cook for 6 minutes on each side, until chicken is cooked thoroughly. Remove from grill and cool. Slice thinly on the diagonal and set aside.

In a large bowl, toss together chèvre, mixed salad greens and roasted pecans and dressing, using as much or as little as you would like. Divide equally over 6 plates.

Arrange chicken slices on each plate of greens and garnish with cilantro sprigs.

Ginger Cilantro Dressing

½	10-oz. (284-mL) jar pickled ginger with ½ cup (125 mL) juice	½
3	cloves garlic, minced	3
1 Tbsp.	sambal badjak (see page 80)	15 mL
¼ cup	rice wine vinegar	50 mL
1	bunch cilantro	1

Place all ingredients together in a food processor or blender and process for 30 seconds.

Roasted Pecans

Roasted pecans are so tasty you can serve them on their own as a snack. To make them, heat a non-stick frying pan until hot. Add the pecans and toss for 1 minute. Add ⅓ cup (75 mL) white sugar to pan and shake for about 1 minute. The sugar should be melted and will have turned a golden brown. Add another ⅓ cup (75 mL) of sugar and toss until melted. Tip pan over a baking sheet so that pecans spill out. Allow them to cool on cookie sheet before breaking into smaller pieces. Do not touch until completely cooled!

Warm Asian Chicken Salad

This is a colorful and delicious salad. Feel free to experiment with your favorite vegetables, and for an extra citrus hit... try pink grapefruit instead of oranges.

Serves 6

3	whole chicken breasts, split, skinned and deboned	3
2 Tbsp.	soy sauce	30 mL
2 Tbsp.	hoisin sauce	30 mL
1 Tbsp.	red wine vinegar	15 mL
2 tsp.	Asian chili sauce	10 mL
12	snow peas	12
1	medium zucchini, diced	1
1	carrot, diced	1
1	head broccoli, cut into florets	1
½	head cauliflower, cut into florets	½
½	red pepper, julienned	½
½	yellow pepper, julienned	½
1	bunch watercress, large stems removed, chopped	1
2	Belgian endives, separated	2
2	oranges, peeled and sliced	2
1	15-oz. (425-mL) can baby corn, drained and rinsed	1
1	15-oz. (425-mL) can water chestnuts, drained and rinsed	1
1 recipe	Spicy Sesame Dressing (next page)	1 recipe

In a bowl, mix together soy sauce, hoisin sauce, red wine vinegar and Asian chili sauce. Add chicken to bowl, turning with a fork until each piece is coated in mixture. Cover bowl and marinate for 1 hour.

Preheat oven broiler.

Place chicken on baking sheet and broil 4–5 inches (10–12 cm) from element. Cook for 6 minutes on each side, until chicken is cooked thoroughly. Remove from grill and cool. Slice thinly on the diagonal and set aside.

In a large bowl, mix together all the prepared vegetables and oranges. Mound on a large serving platter. Cover the centre with chicken slices. Drizzle as much or as little dressing over the salad as you would like.

Spicy Sesame Dressing

½ cup	sesame paste	125 mL
2 Tbsp.	harissa or hot chili paste	30 mL
2 Tbsp.	soy sauce	30 mL
2 Tbsp.	oyster sauce	30 mL
4	cloves garlic, minced	4
	1 inch (2.5 cm) ginger, slivered finely	
¼ tsp.	salt	1 mL
¼ tsp.	black pepper	1 mL
1 Tbsp.	brown sugar	15 mL
4 Tbsp.	vegetable oil	60 mL
4 Tbsp.	water	60 mL

Blend all the ingredients together in a blender or food processor. With motor running, slowly add oil in a thin, steady stream.

Harissa is a hot flavored Tunisian and Moroccan condiment. Some Tunisians eat it with almost everything but I use it for couscous and in this dish.

If you want to make your own harissa, simply grind together 1 tsp. (5 mL) caraway seeds, ½ tsp. (2 mL) salt, 2 Tbsp. (30 mL) cayenne, 1 Tbsp. (15 mL) cumin and 2 cloves garlic in a food processor or blender. Then add ½ cup (125 mL) olive oil in a slow steady stream. Refrigerate for up to 1 month.

Japanese Chicken Salad

T̤ his salad looks gorgeous as the focal point for a special lunch.

Serves 4 to 6

2	whole chicken breasts, split, skinned and deboned, then cut into 1- x ¼-inch (2.5- x .6-cm) strips	2
2 Tbsp.	vegetable oil	30 mL
1 Tbsp.	dry sherry	15 mL
1 Tbsp.	sesame oil	15 mL
4 Tbsp.	rice vinegar	60 mL
4 Tbsp.	soy sauce	60 mL
1½ tsp.	wasabi (Japanese mustard)	7 mL
1 tsp.	minced ginger	5 mL
1 Tbsp.	cold water	15 mL
1	English cucumber, thinly sliced	1
2	green onions, rinsed and chopped	2
1 Tbsp.	toasted sesame seeds	15 mL

Sauté chicken in oil in a skillet over medium heat for 2–3 minutes until chicken is cooked and color becomes opaque. Remove from skillet with a slotted spoon and put in a bowl.

Drizzle sherry over the chicken.

Combine the sesame oil, rice vinegar, soy sauce, wasabi, ginger and cold water in a separate bowl. Add to the chicken and mix together.

Completely cover a serving platter with cucumber slices, then top with the chicken.

Garnish with chopped green onions and toasted sesame seeds. To add more color, try using half toasted black sesame seeds. The combination of the two kinds of seed is very dramatic.

Roast Chicken

A good roasting chicken weighs usually between $3\frac{1}{2}$ and $5\frac{1}{2}$ pounds (1.6 and 2.5 kg). It is tender and very meaty.

In this chapter, I have included a variety of stuffings and bastes. The recipes that require basting use the French method of cooking, which starts with high heat to sear the meat and seal the juices, then lowers the temperature for the duration of the cooking time. Otherwise, I have suggested cooking at a lower, even temperature for self-basting.

Before using any of these recipes, remember the following:

1. Do **not** pack the cavity tightly when stuffing, as the stuffing will expand while cooking.

2. You can bake extra raw stuffing in a baking dish covered with aluminum foil.

3. Leftover stuffing and chicken should be stored separately and used within a few days. The chicken can be frozen for later use.

Mama Rozzie's Challah-Stuffed Chicken

This is Mama Rozzie's holiday special. In her books, every Friday night is a holiday!

Serves 4 to 6

1	4-5-lb. (2-2.5-kg) roasting chicken	1
2 Tbsp.	vegetable oil	30 mL
2	cloves garlic, crushed	2
1 tsp.	onion powder	5 mL
1 tsp.	paprika	5 mL
½ tsp.	Worcestershire sauce	2 mL
	freshly ground black pepper to taste	
1 recipe	Challah Stuffing (next page)	1 recipe

Preheat oven to 375°F (190°C).

Scald chicken with boiling water inside and out, then wash thoroughly with cold water and pat dry with paper towels.

Combine vegetable oil, garlic, onion powder, paprika, Worcestershire sauce and pepper to make a paste. Rub into the cavity and skin of chicken.

Fill the cavity with Challah Stuffing, but do not pack tightly.

Put chicken in a roasting pan and roast for 2–2½ hours. Test for doneness. Chicken is cooked when juices run clear (not pink) when thigh is pricked with a fork; when drumstick moves easily out of thigh joint; and when meat is tender when cut.

Transfer chicken to a serving platter; let rest for 10 minutes before carving.

Challah Stuffing

2	white onions, diced	2
1	carrot, peeled and grated	1
8	stalks celery, finely chopped	8
2 cups	cleaned, sliced mushrooms	500 mL
1	green pepper, seeded and chopped	1
2	cloves garlic, minced	2
3 Tbsp.	vegetable oil	45 mL
3 Tbsp.	unsalted butter	45 mL
3½ cups	stale challah (egg bread), broken into pieces, then soaked in water and the water squeezed out	875 mL
2 tsp.	dried sage leaves	10 mL
	salt and freshly ground black pepper to taste	
2	eggs, lightly beaten	2

Sauté vegetables and garlic in oil and butter in a large skillet over medium heat until softened, about 8 minutes. Remove from skillet to a large bowl.

Add remaining ingredients to bowl and mix together thoroughly.

Roast Chicken Français

Serve this simple French roast chicken with steamed asparagus and oven-roasted potatoes with rosemary.

1	3½-4-lb. (1.75-2-kg) roasting chicken	1
2 Tbsp.	unsalted butter	30 mL
	freshly ground black pepper to taste	
	salt and freshly ground black pepper to taste	
2 Tbsp.	vegetable oil	30 mL
2 Tbsp.	unsalted butter	30 mL
½ cup	water, chicken stock or white wine (optional, for gravy, next page)	125 mL

Preheat oven to 400°F (200°C).

Scald chicken with boiling water inside and out, then wash thoroughly with cold water and pat dry with paper towels.

Mix 2 Tbsp. (30 mL) butter and pepper together and rub into the cavity of the chicken.

Season skin with salt and pepper.

Heat oil and butter in large ovenproof casserole dish and set chicken on its side in the bottom. Cook over medium-high heat until browned, then turn chicken on its other side and cook until browned. Turn chicken breast-side up and cook until browned. Do not let oil burn. Reduce heat, if necessary. Baste with pan juices and cover casserole dish.

Roast the chicken in the oven for 1 hour. Test for doneness. Chicken is cooked when juices run clear (not pink) when thigh is pricked with a fork; when drumstick moves easily out of thigh joint; and when meat is tender when cut.

Transfer chicken to a serving platter and let rest for 5–10 minutes before carving.

Pan Gravy

To make a gravy, degrease pan juices. Add a small amount of liquid (cold water or chicken stock) to the pan and bring to a boil, scraping up the browned bits from the bottom of the pan. Deglaze with ½ cup (125 mL) water, chicken stock or white wine. Slowly add and stir.

Once all the liquid has been added to the gravy, boil until thickened, then remove from heat and finish with the addition of 1 Tbsp. (15 mL) butter or fresh herbs. Season with salt and pepper to taste.

Lazy Gourmet Roast Chicken with Wild Rice Stuffing

T his stuffing is very popular at The Lazy Gourmet, a popular bistro/ catering company in Vancouver. It can be used to stuff salmon as well.

Serves 4 to 6

1	4–5-lb. (2–2.5-kg) roasting chicken	1
	freshly ground black pepper to taste	
1 recipe	Wild Rice Stuffing (next page)	1 recipe
1 tsp.	finely chopped fresh parsley	5 mL
1 tsp.	onion powder	5 mL
1 tsp.	garlic powder	5 mL
	salt and freshly ground black pepper to taste	

Preheat oven to 375°F (190°C).

Scald chicken with boiling water inside and out, then wash thoroughly with cold water and pat dry with paper towels.

Season cavity of chicken with pepper. Fill the cavity with Wild Rice Stuffing, but do not pack tightly.

Mix parsley, onion powder, garlic powder, salt and pepper together and season skin with the mixture.

Put chicken in a roasting pan and roast for 2–2½ hours. Test for doneness. Chicken is cooked when juices run clear (not pink) when thigh is pricked with a fork; when drumstick moves easily out of thigh joint; and when meat is tender when cut.

Transfer chicken to a serving platter and let rest for 5–10 minutes before carving.

Wild Rice Stuffing

2	cloves garlic, minced	2
1 Tbsp.	minced ginger	15 mL
3 Tbsp.	unsalted butter	45 mL
1	large white onion, chopped	1
4	stalks celery, chopped	4
½ lb.	mushrooms, cleaned and sliced	250 g
¼ cup	seeded, chopped green pepper	50 mL
6	slices stale bread, broken into pieces	6
1 cup	cooked wild rice	250 mL
1 cup	cooked white rice	250 mL
1 cup	chopped water chestnuts	250 mL
⅓ cup	soy sauce	75 mL
¼ cup	sherry	50 mL
2 tsp.	ground rosemary	10 mL
1 tsp.	dried basil leaves	5 mL
1 tsp.	dried thyme leaves	5 mL
	salt and freshly ground black pepper to taste	

Sauté garlic and ginger in butter in a skillet over medium heat for 1 minute.

Add onion, celery, mushrooms and green pepper to skillet and sauté for 3–5 minutes, until vegetables are soft. Remove from skillet to a large bowl.

Add stale bread to vegetables in bowl and let bread soak up the pan juices.

Add remaining ingredients to bowl and mix together thoroughly.

Zonda's Quick Mustard Chicken

*ere it is, B.G.!
David and
Zonda brought
this to the first
edition, and it's so
good, we had to
include it again.*

Serves 2 to 4

1	2½–3-lb. (1.25–1.5-kg) roasting chicken	1
	salt and freshly ground black pepper to taste	
¼ cup	Dijon mustard	50 mL
1	whole lemon	1
2	slices bacon	2
1 tsp.	dried rosemary leaves (optional)	5 mL
6	small potatoes, scrubbed and quartered (optional)	6
3	carrots, peeled and cut in chunks (optional)	3
2	small white onions, halved (optional)	2

Preheat oven to 400°F (200°C).

Scald chicken with boiling water inside and out, then wash thoroughly with cold water and pat dry with paper towels.

Season cavity and skin of chicken with salt and pepper. Slather skin with mustard.

Put lemon in cavity and place chicken in clay pot which has been soaked in water according to the manufacturer's instructions.

Lay 1 slice of bacon lengthwise down each breast. Sprinkle chicken with rosemary, if desired.

Put vegetables around chicken in pot, if desired.

Cover pot and roast for 1¼ hours.

Remove cover from pot and roast for an additional 15 minutes. Test for doneness. Chicken is cooked when juices run clear (not pink) when thigh is pricked with a fork; when drumstick moves easily out of thigh joint; and when meat is tender when cut.

Transfer chicken to a serving platter and let rest for 5–10 minutes before carving. Serve with roasted vegetables.

Roast Chicken Israeli-Style

This chicken is delicious on its own. However, when you add the Ginger Orange Sauce, you can almost smell the cedars of Jerusalem.

Serves 4 to 6

1	4–5-lb. (2–2.5-kg) roasting chicken	1
2 Tbsp.	unsalted butter	30 mL
3 Tbsp.	liquid honey	45 mL
1 tsp.	paprika	5 mL
1 tsp.	salt	5 mL
1 cup	freshly squeezed orange juice	250 mL
1 recipe	Ginger Orange Sauce (next page)	1 recipe

Preheat oven to 400°F (200°C).

Scald chicken with boiling water inside and out, then wash thoroughly with cold water and pat dry with paper towels.

In a small saucepan, mix together butter, honey, paprika and salt. Heat until butter has melted. Coat cavity and skin of chicken with this mixture.

Put chicken in a roasting pan and pour orange juice over chicken.

Put roasting pan in oven and immediately reduce heat to 350°F (180°C). Roast for 2½–3 hours, basting often with pan juices.

Thirty minutes before chicken is finished roasting, prepare the sauce.

Test for doneness. Chicken is cooked when juices run clear (not pink) when thigh is pricked with a fork; when drumstick moves easily out of thigh joint; and when meat is tender when cut.

Transfer chicken to a serving platter and let rest for 5–10 minutes before carving. Serve with Ginger Orange Sauce on the side.

Ginger Orange Sauce

1 cup	freshly squeezed orange juice	250 mL
1 tsp.	grated orange peel	5 mL
2	green onions, rinsed and chopped	2
¼ cup	seeded, chopped green pepper	50 mL
1 tsp.	minced ginger	5 mL
½ tsp.	horseradish	2 mL
1 tsp.	cornstarch	5 mL

Combine all ingredients except cornstarch in a saucepan. Bring to a boil, reduce heat to low and simmer for 15 minutes. Keep hot.

Just before serving, dissolve cornstarch in 1 Tbsp. (15 mL) cold water. Add to saucepan and whisk in. Simmer over low heat, about 5 minutes until sauce thickens somewhat.

Middle Eastern-Style Capon

When my cousin Arthur first made this for dinner, I knew I had to include it—I hope you'll agree!

Serves 6 to 8

1	7-lb. (3.5-kg) capon	1
1 recipe	Raisin Bulgur Stuffing (next page)	1 recipe
½ cup	liquid honey	125 mL
2 Tbsp.	unsalted butter	30 mL
½ tsp.	salt	2 mL
6 Tbsp.	sesame seeds	90 mL

Preheat oven to 400°F (200°C).

Scald capon with boiling water inside and out, then wash thoroughly with cold water and pat dry with paper towels.

Fill the cavity with stuffing, but do not pack tightly.

Combine honey, butter and salt in a small saucepan, and heat over medium heat until butter has melted.

Put capon in a roasting pan and baste with this mixture.

Put roasting pan in oven and immediately reduce heat to 350°F (180°C). Roast for 2¼ hours, basting often with pan juices.

After 2¼ hours, sprinkle sesame seeds over capon and roast for an additional 15 minutes. Test for doneness. Capon is cooked when juices run clear (not pink) when thigh is pricked with a fork; when drumstick moves easily out of thigh joint; and when meat is tender when cut.

Transfer capon to a serving platter and let rest for 5–10 minutes before carving.

Raisin Bulgur Stuffing

1	large white onion, chopped	1
2 Tbsp.	unsalted butter	30 mL
1 cup	bulgur wheat	250 mL
1½ cups	Chicken Stock (page 32)	375 mL
2 Tbsp.	freshly squeezed lemon juice	30 mL
½ cup	dark seedless raisins	125 mL
½ cup	golden seedless raisins	125 mL
1 tsp.	ground cinnamon	5 mL
¼ tsp.	salt	1 mL
	freshly ground black pepper to taste	

Sauté onion in butter in a large skillet over medium heat until soft, about 4–6 minutes.

Add bulgur wheat to skillet and sauté over medium heat for 5 minutes.

Add remaining ingredients to skillet. Bring to a boil, reduce heat to low, then cover and simmer for 5 minutes. Remove from heat and let stand, covered, for 1 hour.

Thai Roasted Chicken

This flavorful dish can be served with a noodle salad and roasted vegetables. For dessert, try something light, like a delicious lemon tart with cookies.

Serves 4 to 6

1	3½–4-lb. (1.75–2-kg) chicken	1
½ tsp.	salt	2 mL
1 Tbsp.	ground ginger	15 mL
1 Tbsp.	paprika	15 mL
¼ tsp.	cayenne	1 mL
1 recipe	Ginger Mushroom Stuffing (next page)	1 recipe
¼ cup	butter	50 mL
2 Tbsp.	honey	30 mL
1 Tbsp.	mirin seasoning (see next page)	15 mL
2 Tbsp.	soy sauce	30 mL

Preheat oven to 375°F (190°C).

Scald chicken with boiling water inside and out, then wash thoroughly with cold water and pat dry with paper towels.

Combine salt, ginger, paprika and cayenne in a small bowl. Rub chicken inside and out with spice mixture.

Spoon the Ginger Mushroom Stuffing into the cavity of the chicken. Place in roasting pan, and bake for 1¼ hours.

Melt butter, honey, mirin seasoning and soy sauce together in a bowl in the microwave oven or in a small heavy saucepan over low heat on top of the stove.

Remove chicken from oven, baste thoroughly with sauce, and increase temperature to 400°F (200°C) for an additional 5 minutes. Test for doneness. Chicken is done when juices run clear (not pink) when thigh is pricked with a fork; when drumstick moves easily out of joint; and when meat is tender when cut.

Baste again, remove to a platter and let rest for 5–10 minutes before carving.

MIRIN SEASONING:

Mirin seasoning is a combination of rice wine (mirin) and cornstarch. You can use this, or plain mirin (even sherry can be used in a pinch) in this recipe. I prefer the mirin seasoning because it adds an extra shine to the roasted chicken.

Ginger Mushroom Stuffing

1	16-oz. (455-mL) can straw mushrooms	1
1 Tbsp.	fresh ginger, finely sliced	15 mL
¼ tsp.	salt	1 mL
1	white onion, chopped	1

Drain the liquid from the straw mushrooms, then put the mushrooms in a saucepan with 5 cups (1.2 L) cold water. Bring to a boil, then reduce heat and simmer for 30 minutes. Drain again.

Add ginger, salt and onion to the mushrooms and mix thoroughly.

Asian Roast Chicken with Vegetable Rice Stuffing

This dish is very rich, so serve it with some Asian greens, lightly steamed, and dinner's ready.

Serves 4 to 6

1	4–5-lb. (2–2.5-kg) roasting chicken	1
1 recipe	Vegetable Rice Stuffing (next page)	1 recipe
½ cup	ketchup	125 mL
2 Tbsp.	soy sauce	30 mL
2 Tbsp.	dry sherry	30 mL
1 Tbsp.	hot chili oil (next page)	15 mL
1 Tbsp.	hoisin sauce	15 mL

Preheat oven to 400°F (200°C).

Scald chicken with boiling water inside and out, then wash thoroughly with cold water and pat dry with paper towels.

Fill the cavity with Vegetable Rice Stuffing, but do not pack tightly.

In a small bowl, combine ketchup, soy sauce, sherry, chili oil and hoisin sauce.

Put chicken in a roasting pan and baste with this mixture.

Roast chicken for 15 minutes, then reduce heat to 325°F (160°C) and roast for 2–2½ hours, basting often with pan juices. Test for doneness. Chicken is cooked when juices run clear (not pink) when thigh is pricked with a fork; when drumstick moves easily out of thigh joint; and when meat is tender when cut.

Transfer chicken to a serving platter and let rest for 5–10 minutes before carving.

Vegetable Rice Stuffing

1	clove garlic, minced	1
1 tsp.	minced ginger	5 mL
2 Tbsp.	vegetable oil	30 mL
2 Tbsp.	unsalted butter	30 mL
½ cup	diced white onion	25 mL
2	green onions, rinsed and cut into ½-inch (1-cm) pieces	2
1 cup	diced celery	250 mL
⅓ cup	seeded, diced green pepper	75 mL
1 cup	cooked rice	250 mL
1	8-oz. (230-mL) can water chestnuts, drained and sliced	1
2 Tbsp.	soy sauce	30 mL
2 Tbsp.	cold water	30 mL
1 tsp.	sugar	5 mL
	freshly ground black pepper to taste	
2 Tbsp.	sherry	30 mL

Sauté garlic and ginger in oil and butter in a skillet over medium heat for 1 minute.

Add white onion, green onions, celery, green pepper, rice and water chestnuts, and sauté over medium heat for 3 minutes.

Add soy sauce, water, sugar and pepper, stirring constantly until blended in.

Stir in sherry, cover and cook for 1 minute, then remove skillet from heat.

HOT CHILI OIL:
Hot chili oil is available in most Asian markets—or make your own. To prepare it, just put 6 Tbsp. (90 mL) peanut or vegetable oil in a small saucepan over medium heat. When hot, add 8–10 red chili peppers or 2 Tbsp. (30 mL) dried chilies to oil and simmer over low heat, stirring occasionally, until oil turns dark red. Cool and strain. Store in a glass bottle in the refrigerator for up to 2 weeks.

Five-Spice Roasted Chicken with Vegetable Stuffing

Five-spice powder is made of star anise, anise pepper (sometimes called Szechuan peppercorns), fennel, cloves and cinnamon. The powder must be used sparingly because it is pungent.

Serves 4 to 6

1	3½–4-lb. (1.75–2.5-kg) chicken	1
1 Tbsp.	salt	15 mL
1 Tbsp.	5-spice powder	15 mL
1 recipe	Vegetable Stuffing (next page)	1 recipe
4 Tbsp.	butter, unsalted	60 mL
2 Tbsp.	liquid honey	30 mL
¼ cup	cilantro leaves	50 mL

Preheat oven to 375°F (190°C).

Scald chicken with boiling water inside and out, then wash thoroughly with cold water and pat dry with paper towels. Trim any excess fat from chicken.

Mix together salt and 5-spice powder and rub into the cavity and skin of chicken.

Spoon Vegetable Stuffing into the cavity.

Place chicken in a roasting pan and bake for 1 hour and 10 minutes.

Melt butter and honey together in a small saucepan. Increase oven temperature to 400°F (200°C). Remove chicken from oven and baste with honey-butter. Return chicken to oven and bake at 400°F (200°C) for 5 minutes. Test for doneness. Chicken is cooked when juices run clear (not pink) when thigh is pricked with a fork; when drumstick moves easily out of thigh joint; and when meat is tender when cut.

Remove chicken from oven and baste again.

Transfer chicken to a serving platter and let rest for 5–10 minutes before carving. Garnish with cilantro and serve.

Vegetable Stuffing

2 cups	potatoes, peeled and quartered	500 mL
¼ cup	carrots, thinly sliced	50 mL
¼ cup	snow peas, sliced on the diagonal	50 mL
¼ cup	straw mushrooms, drained and halved	50 mL
¼ tsp.	salt	1 mL

Place potatoes in a pot with enough cold water to cover. Bring to a boil, reduce heat to medium, and cook for about 10 minutes, until just cooked.

Remove pot and combine with remaining ingredients.

Sephardi Clay-Baked Roast Chicken

This Mediterranean dish is delicious with rice pilaf and a steamed green vegetable. If you don't have a clay pot, see the directions on the next page.

Serves 4 to 6

1	4–5-lb. (2–2.5-kg) roasting chicken	1
2 tsp.	salt	10 mL
2 tsp.	freshly ground pepper	10 mL
1	lemon	1
8	sprigs fresh thyme	8
8	cloves garlic, peeled	8
3 Tbsp.	olive oil	45 mL
⅔ cup	freshly squeezed lemon juice	150 mL
	fresh thyme sprigs	

To prepare clay pot for baking, soak entire pot in hot water for 15 minutes. Remove from water but do not dry.

Scald chicken with boiling water inside and out, then wash thoroughly with cold water and pat dry with paper towels.

Sprinkle cavity of chicken with half of the salt and pepper.

Cut lemon in half and place in cavity of chicken.

Add 3 sprigs of thyme and 2 cloves of garlic in the cavity of the chicken.

Rub 1 garlic clove around outside of chicken and then sprinkle with salt and pepper.

Place chicken in clay pot and surround with remaining garlic and thyme.

Combine olive oil and lemon juice and pour over chicken.

Cover clay pot and place into cold oven. Cooking must start in a cold oven or the clay pot could crack during cooking. Turn the oven to 450°F (230°C) and cook for 15 minutes.

Reduce temperature to 350°F (180°C) and cook for 1½ hours. Test for doneness. Chicken is cooked when juices run clear (not pink) when thigh is pricked with a fork; when drumstick moves easily out of joint; and when meat is tender when cut.

Carve, decorate with thyme sprigs and serve with spinach orzo and yellow beans.

If you don't own a clay pot, you will miss out on the fabulous aroma that greets the cook upon opening it. However, you can still prepare this dish. Simply preheat the oven to 450°F (230°C). Place chicken in an uncovered roasting pan and roast for 20 minutes. Reduce heat to 350°F (180°C), cover roasting pan and continue roasting for 1 hour. Uncover pot for 20 minutes longer and test for doneness.

Salt-Buried Chicken

The traditional Chinese recipe for salt-buried chicken uses only salt and chicken. This recipe is a Cantonese adaptation. Serve it as part of a Chinese feast!

Serves 2 to 4

1	2–3-lb. (1–1.5-kg) roasting chicken	1
2 Tbsp.	soy sauce	30 mL
2 Tbsp.	brandy	30 mL
2	green onions, rinsed and cut into 2-inch (5-cm) pieces	2
2 tsp.	minced ginger	10 mL
2 Tbsp.	dried chopped tangerine peel	30 mL
7 lbs.	coarse salt	3.5 kg

Wash chicken thoroughly with cold water and dry overnight, covered with plastic wrap, in refrigerator.

Preheat oven to 375°F (190°C).

Mix soy sauce, brandy, green onions, ginger and peel together and spoon into cavity of chicken.

Put salt in the bottom of a large ovenproof casserole dish and heat in oven for 15 minutes.

When salt is heated through, make a hole in the middle of the dish. Place the chicken in the hole. Bury the chicken in salt.

Cover casserole dish and cook over low heat on the stovetop for 10 minutes, then roast for 1 hour in the oven.

Remove casserole dish from oven, break salt away from chicken and discard. Transfer chicken to a serving platter and let rest for 5–10 minutes before carving.

Baked Chicken

The one thing that all the recipes in this chapter have in common is ease of preparation. The glazes are simple and the baking process requires little interruption. Many of the recipes use fryers, which are 2½–3½ lb. (1.25–1.75 kg) chickens, but if you have picky eaters, substitute their favorite part of the chicken. Most of the recipes are delicious reheated—in fact, I love Lyla's Cranberry Chicken even better the second day—so feel free to double the recipes and freeze for another day. Then, on those days when you're just too busy or too tired to cook, simply defrost, reheat and serve.

Pecan Chicken

Feel free to substitute almonds or peanuts. Because this dish is very rich your guests will appreciate it if the rest of the meal is light and simple.

Serves 6

¾ cup	potato starch	175 mL
1½ tsp.	paprika	7 mL
1 tsp.	salt	5 mL
	freshly ground black pepper to taste	
2	2½-lb. (1.25-kg) fryers, quartered	2
1	egg, lightly beaten	1
3 Tbsp.	milk	50 mL
1 Tbsp.	Dijon mustard	15 mL
1½ cups	finely chopped toasted pecans	375 mL
3 Tbsp.	light vegetable oil	45 mL
1 recipe	Mustard Sauce (next page)	1 recipe

Preheat oven to 375°F (190°C).

Mix potato starch, paprika, salt and pepper in a bowl.

Blend egg, milk and mustard in a bowl.

Dredge chicken, one piece at a time, in the spice mixture, then dip in egg mixture, shaking off the excess.

Roll chicken pieces in pecans until they are completely covered, then put chicken in a roasting pan skin side down. Drizzle oil over chicken.

Bake for 30 minutes on each side, until chicken is cooked thoroughly.

Transfer chicken to a serving platter or individual plates. Serve with Mustard Sauce on the side.

Mustard Sauce

2 Tbsp.	unsalted butter	30 mL
2 Tbsp.	flour	30 mL
1 cup	scalded milk	250 mL
2 Tbsp.	Dijon or tarragon mustard	30 mL
	salt and freshly ground black pepper to taste	

Melt butter in a skillet over medium heat. Do not brown.

Add flour, stirring constantly with a whisk, and cook for 1 minute.

Add scalded milk all at once, stirring constantly with a whisk until sauce thickens, about 7–10 minutes, then simmer for 5 minutes, stirring occasionally.

Whisk in mustard, salt and pepper.

Lyla's Cranberry Chicken

I double this recipe because it's particularly tasty the second time around. It's great reheated—the sauce gets thick and sticky and the chicken is more flavorful. Serve with plain rice—your guests will want to scoop the sauce on top.

Serves 6

2	2½-lb. (1.25-kg) fryers, quartered	2
1 tsp.	onion powder	5 mL
1 tsp.	garlic powder	5 mL
1	14-oz. (398-mL) can whole cranberry sauce	1
3 Tbsp.	soy sauce	45 mL
3 Tbsp.	frozen orange juice concentrate	45 mL
3 Tbsp.	brown sugar	45 mL
1 tsp.	minced ginger	5 mL
2 Tbsp.	sesame seeds	30 mL

Preheat oven to 375°F (190°C).

Put chicken, skin side up, in a roasting pan and season with onion powder and garlic powder.

Bake for 15 minutes, remove from oven and drain pan juices. Return chicken to roasting pan.

While chicken is baking, combine the remaining ingredients, except the sesame seeds, in a saucepan. Bring to a boil, reduce heat to low and simmer for 10 minutes. Spread cranberry sauce evenly over chicken, and sprinkle with sesame seeds.

Bake chicken for another 45 minutes. Increase temperature to broil and set the roasting pan 6 inches (15 cm) from element. Broil until the chicken is dark and sticky, about 5–8 minutes.

Transfer chicken to a serving platter or individual plates.

Chicken with Sour Cream and Sherry

This is so easy, so fast, so tasty! It's also the only chicken dish my husband Ira has ever prepared for me. To update it, use oyster mushrooms; and for a lower-fat version, use light sour cream or half sour cream, half yogurt.

Serves 4 to 6

3	whole chicken breasts, split	3
1 cup	sour cream	250 mL
1	small can golden mushroom soup	1
½ cup	dry sherry	125 mL
¼ lb.	cleaned, sliced mushrooms	125 g

Preheat oven to 375°F (190°C).

Put chicken, skin side up, in a 9- x 13-inch (22- x 34-cm) baking dish.

Mix sour cream, mushroom soup and sherry in a bowl, then pour over chicken.

Distribute mushrooms over chicken.

Bake for 1–1¼ hours, until chicken is cooked thoroughly.

Transfer chicken to a serving platter or individual plates.

Dijon Chicken

If you like mustard, you'll love this! For a change, try some of the herbed Dijon-style mustards.

Serves 4 to 6

½ cup	Dijon mustard	125 mL
2 Tbsp.	vegetable oil	30 mL
4	green onions, rinsed and finely chopped	4
½ tsp.	dried tarragon leaves	2 mL
¼ tsp.	hot pepper sauce	1 mL
3	whole chicken breasts, split and skinned	3
¾ cup	breadcrumbs	175 mL
3 Tbsp.	vegetable oil	45 mL

Preheat oven to 375°F (190°C).

Combine mustard, oil, green onions, tarragon and hot pepper sauce in a bowl.

Add chicken, one piece at a time, to mustard mixture and coat well.

Dredge chicken pieces in breadcrumbs, then put in a roasting pan. Drizzle oil over chicken.

Bake for 1 hour, until chicken is cooked thoroughly.

Transfer chicken to a serving platter or individual plates.

Gail's Easy Tarragon Chicken

ousin Gail shared this family favorite. I trust every recipe from her kitchen. Be sure to make extra because this is delicious cold!

Serves 6

2	2½-lb. (1.25-kg) fryers, quartered	2
½ cup	honey mustard	125 mL
2	cloves garlic, crushed	2
2 tsp.	dried tarragon leaves	10 mL
	salt and freshly ground black pepper to taste	
3 Tbsp.	toasted sesame seeds	45 mL

Preheat oven to broil.

Combine honey mustard, garlic, tarragon leaves, salt and pepper in a bowl and brush over chicken.

Put chicken, skin side up, in a roasting pan. Broil until skin is crispy, about 3–5 minutes. Reduce heat to 350°F (180°C) and bake for 45 minutes, then remove pan from oven.

Sprinkle sesame seeds over chicken, return pan to oven and bake for an additional 10–15 minutes, until chicken is cooked thoroughly.

Transfer chicken to a serving platter or individual plates.

Richard's Hard-Knock Chicken

I haven't seen Richard and Jane for years but when I make this dish I think of them fondly. Sometimes I use slices of this dish as an hors d'oeuvre.

Serves 4 to 6

3	whole chicken breasts, split, skinned and deboned	3
	salt and freshly ground black pepper to taste	
¼ cup	Dijon mustard	50 mL
1 recipe	Zucchini Filling (next page)	1 recipe
3 Tbsp.	unsalted butter	45 mL
	pinch dried basil	
4–6	sprigs of fresh parsley	4–6

Preheat oven to 350°F (180°C).

Pound chicken breasts between two pieces of waxed paper to a thickness of ⅛ inch (.3 cm).

Season chicken pieces with salt and pepper, then slather with mustard.

Spread with Zucchini Filling.

Roll up chicken pieces and secure each with a toothpick.

Melt butter in a skillet over medium heat. Add a pinch of dried basil, then add chicken rolls and cook until lightly browned, about 3–5 minutes.

Transfer chicken to a 9-inch (22-cm) square baking dish. Bake for 15–20 minutes, until chicken is cooked thoroughly. Remove dish from oven, allow chicken to cool, then remove toothpicks and slice each roll into 3–4 pieces.

Transfer chicken to a serving platter or individual plates. Garnish with sprigs of parsley.

Zucchini Filling

1	medium white onion, finely chopped	1
2 Tbsp.	unsalted butter	30 mL
3	cloves garlic, minced	3
3	medium zucchini, grated and the liquid drained	3
1 Tbsp.	dried thyme leaves	15 mL
	salt and freshly ground black pepper to taste	
1½ Tbsp.	toasted pine nuts	20 mL
1½ Tbsp.	freshly grated Parmesan cheese	20 mL
½ cup	herbed cream cheese	125 mL

Sauté onion in butter in a skillet over medium heat for 2 minutes.

Add garlic and cook for 1–2 minutes more.

Add zucchini and thyme leaves and cook 5 minutes more.

Season with salt and pepper, then transfer contents of skillet to a bowl.

Add pine nuts and cheeses and mix together thoroughly.

Grandma Faye's Baked Chicken with Apricot Glaze

Grandma Faye used to make this for special family dinners. It is still a favorite at my house. It's easy to prepare and delicious to eat. I sometimes sprinkle toasted sesame seeds over the chicken for the last 15 minutes of baking.

Serves 6

2	2½-lb. (1.25-kg) fryers, quartered	2
	salt and freshly ground black pepper to taste	
1 tsp.	onion powder	5 mL
1 tsp.	garlic powder	5 mL
1 cup	apricot preserves	250 mL
½ cup	chili sauce	125 mL
¼ cup	dry red wine	50 mL
2 Tbsp.	soy sauce	30 mL
2 Tbsp.	liquid honey	30 mL
1 tsp.	minced ginger	5 mL
	salt to taste	

Preheat oven to 375°F (190°C).

Put chicken, skin side up, in a roasting pan.

Season with salt, pepper, onion powder and garlic powder.

Combine remaining ingredients in a bowl, then spread evenly over chicken.

Bake for 1 hour, until chicken is cooked thoroughly.

Transfer chicken to a serving platter or individual plates.

Chicken Kiev–Variations on a Theme

You don't have to live in Kiev to like this dish. Feel free to experiment with the flavors your family enjoys.

Serves 6 to 8

4	whole chicken breasts, split, skinned and deboned	4
	salt and freshly ground black pepper to taste	
8 Tbsp.	flavored butter of your choice (pages 120–21)	120 mL
¾ cup	flour	175 mL
3	eggs, lightly beaten	3
¾ cup	corn flake crumbs	175 mL
½ tsp.	ground rosemary	2 mL

Pound chicken breasts between two pieces of waxed paper to a thickness of ¼ inch (.6 cm). Season chicken with salt and pepper.

Put 1 Tbsp. (15 mL) flavored butter on each chicken breast.

Roll up chicken pieces and secure each with a toothpick. Chill in refrigerator for 1 hour.

Preheat oven to 375°F (190°C).

Put flour and eggs in separate bowls, and mix corn flakes and rosemary in a third bowl.

Dredge chicken in flour, then dip in egg, shaking off excess. Roll chicken in crumb mixture until completely covered.

Put chicken in a 9-inch (22-cm) square baking dish. Bake for 20 minutes until chicken is cooked thoroughly. Alternatively, use the traditional method and heat oil in a deep fryer to 360°F (185°C), then fry the chicken in hot oil for 10–12 minutes until browned and cooked through. Remove chicken from deep fryer with tongs and drain on paper towels. Transfer chicken to a serving platter or individual plates.

Lime Ginger Butter

½ cup	unsalted butter, softened	125 mL
2 Tbsp.	freshly squeezed lime juice	30 mL
2 tsp.	minced ginger	10 mL
¼ cup	finely chopped fresh cilantro	50 mL
	salt to taste	

Mustard Butter

½ cup	unsalted butter, softened	125 mL
2 Tbsp.	Dijon mustard	30 mL
1 tsp.	freshly squeezed lemon juice	5 mL
2	cloves garlic, crushed	2
2 Tbsp.	finely chopped fresh parsley	30 mL
2 Tbsp.	finely chopped fresh dill	30 mL

Shallot Tarragon Butter

½ cup	unsalted butter, softened	125 mL
3	shallots, minced	3
2 tsp.	dried tarragon leaves	10 mL
	salt and freshly ground black pepper to taste	

Basil Butter

½ cup	unsalted butter, softened	125 mL
¼ cup	finely chopped fresh basil	50 mL
1 tsp.	tomato paste	5 mL
2	cloves garlic, crushed	2
	salt and freshly ground black pepper to taste	

Parsley Butter

½ cup	unsalted butter, softened	125 mL
¼ cup	finely chopped fresh parsley	50 mL
1 Tbsp.	freshly squeezed lemon juice	15 mL
	freshly ground black pepper to taste	

To make flavored butters, combine ingredients in a bowl, then place on waxed paper, and roll into a log. Wrap and chill in refrigerator, or for longer storage, keep in freezer for up to 3 months.

I use a food processor to make these butters. I use them to add flavor to a variety of dishes that call for butter—for example, scrambled eggs with basil butter!

Chicken Marvelosa

This one marinates overnight.

This is rich in flavor and reminiscent of a Greek isle. Serve it with a mild saffron rice and a green vegetable, such as spinach. Mother Roz hates olives but loves this.

Serves 6

2	2½-lb. (1.25-kg) fryers, quartered	2
1 recipe	Herbed Apricot Marinade (next page)	1 recipe
¾ cup	dry white wine	175 mL
¾ cup	brown sugar	175 mL
1 Tbsp.	finely chopped fresh cilantro	15 mL

Arrange chicken, skin side up, in a single layer in a roasting pan.

Spoon Herbed Apricot Marinade over chicken, cover and put in the refrigerator overnight.

Preheat oven to 375°F (190°C).

Remove chicken from refrigerator, leaving the marinade on the chicken. Pour dry white wine over top and sprinkle brown sugar over chicken.

Bake for 1 hour, until chicken is cooked thoroughly.

Transfer chicken to a serving platter or individual plates. Garnish with cilantro.

Herbed Apricot Marinade

½ cup	olive oil	125 mL
½ cup	red wine vinegar	125 mL
⅓ cup	minced garlic	75 mL
½ cup	capers, with ⅓ cup (75 mL) liquid	125 mL
½ cup	pitted, sliced green olives	125 mL
2	bay leaves	2
2 Tbsp.	finely chopped fresh parsley	30 mL
1 Tbsp.	dried oregano	15 mL
1 cup	julienned dried apricots	250 mL
2 Tbsp.	apricot preserves	30 mL

Thoroughly combine all ingredients in a bowl.

Matti's Sesame Chicken

atti no longer prepares Friday night dinner at sister Rena's but we continue to enjoy this dish. It's delicious with rice pilaf and steamed broccoli.

Serves 6

2	2½-lb. (1.25-kg) fryers, quartered	2
¼ cup	vegetable oil	50 mL
¼ cup	freshly squeezed lemon juice	50 mL
1 cup	flour	250 mL
¼ cup	toasted sesame seeds (page 7)	50 mL
1 tsp.	finely chopped fresh parsley	5 mL
1 tsp.	dried thyme leaves	5 mL
1 Tbsp.	paprika	15 mL
2 tsp.	salt	10 mL

Preheat oven to 425°F (220°C).

Mix oil and lemon juice in a bowl.

Mix remaining ingredients, except chicken, in a separate bowl.

Dip chicken, one piece at a time, in oil and lemon juice, then dredge in flour mixture.

Put chicken, skin side down, in an oiled 9- x 13-inch (22- x 34-cm) baking dish. Bake for 30 minutes on each side, until chicken is cooked thoroughly.

Transfer chicken to a serving platter or individual plates.

Egyptian Lemon Chicken

*T**he lemon-
marinated
onions are simply
sensational!***

Serves 6 to 8

4	whole chicken breasts, split	4
½ cup	vegetable oil	125 mL
½ cup	freshly squeezed lemon juice	125 mL
2	large white onions, thinly sliced into rings	2
¼ cup	finely chopped fresh parsley	50 mL
2	bay leaves	2
1 tsp.	ground thyme	5 mL
½ tsp.	cayenne	2 mL
1½ tsp.	salt	7 mL
1½ tsp.	coarse black pepper	7 mL
1½ cups	Chicken Stock (page 32)	375 mL

Put chicken, skin side down, in a 9- x 13-inch (22- x 34-cm) baking dish.

Make a marinade by combining remaining ingredients, except chicken stock, in a large bowl. Cover chicken with marinade and put in the refrigerator for 30 minutes to 1 hour.

Preheat oven to broil.

Put chicken, skin side up, on a baking sheet. Broil until skin is lightly browned, about 3–5 minutes. While chicken is cooking, simmer marinade over low heat in a saucepan on top of the stove.

Remove chicken from the oven and reduce heat to 375°F (190°C). Place chicken in baking dish, pour marinade over and add chicken stock. Bake for 30–45 minutes, until chicken is cooked thoroughly.

Transfer chicken to a serving platter or individual plates.

Coconut Chicken

T his dish hits the spot on a cold winter night. Serve with plain rice, so guests can spoon the delicious sauce over their rice.

3	whole chicken breasts, split	3
1 recipe	Garlicky Peanut Paste (next page)	1 recipe
1 Tbsp.	vegetable oil	15 mL
2 Tbsp.	unsalted butter	30 mL
2 cups	coconut cream	500 mL
1 Tbsp.	soy sauce	15 mL
3 Tbsp.	toasted, grated coconut	45 mL
6	sprigs fresh parsley	6

Preheat oven to 375°F (190°C).

Coat chicken with Garlicky Peanut Paste.

Sauté chicken in oil and butter in a skillet over medium heat for 2 minutes on each side. Transfer to a 9- x 13-inch (22- x 34-cm) baking dish, skin side down.

Mix coconut cream and soy sauce in a bowl, adding any remaining paste, then pour over chicken.

Cover dish with aluminum foil and bake for 15 minutes. Turn chicken and cook for an additional 10 minutes, until cooked thoroughly.

Transfer chicken to a serving platter or individual plates. Garnish with toasted coconut and parsley.

Garlicky Peanut Paste

¼ cup	chopped shallots	50 mL
3	cloves garlic, chopped	3
¼ cup	peanuts	50 mL
2 tsp.	freshly squeezed lemon juice	10 mL
2 tsp.	grated lemon peel	10 mL
1 tsp.	sugar	5 mL
1 tsp.	salt	5 mL

Combine all ingredients in a food processor or blender until smooth.

Tandoori Chicken

This one marinates overnight.

Serve with naan *(Indian bread) and raita (yogurt-cucumber salad). This dish derives its name from the tandoor, the oven in which it is baked in India. Due to the cooking process, it is usually bright red. To simulate this, you can add $\frac{1}{4}$ tsp. (1 mL) red food colouring.*
To save time, buy tandoori paste in the Indian section of grocery stores.

Serves 6

2	2½–3-lb. (1.25–1.5-kg) fryers, each cut into 8 pieces	2
⅓ cup	freshly squeezed lime juice	75 mL
2 tsp.	cayenne	10 mL
1 tsp.	salt	5 mL
1 tsp.	freshly ground black pepper	5 mL
1 recipe	Tandoori Paste (next page)	1 recipe
2 cups	yogurt	500 mL
2 Tbsp.	grated coconut	30 mL

Prick chicken with a fork and, using a sharp paring knife, make several ½-inch (2.5-cm) cuts in each piece of chicken.

Mix lime juice, cayenne, salt and pepper in a bowl, then rub into chicken. Let chicken sit for 30 minutes in the refrigerator.

Wearing rubber gloves to prevent hands from staining, rub Tandoori Paste into chicken, then put chicken in a roasting pan.

Rub yogurt into chicken. Cover roasting pan and put in the refrigerator overnight.

Preheat oven to 375°F (190°C).

Bake chicken uncovered for 1 hour, until chicken is cooked thoroughly, then increase heat to broil and cook until skin becomes crispy, about 3–5 minutes.

Transfer chicken to a serving platter or individual plates. Garnish with grated coconut.

Tandoori Paste

2 Tbsp.	yogurt	30 mL
1 Tbsp.	coriander seeds	15 mL
2 Tbsp.	cardamom pods	30 mL
1	medium onion, quartered	1
3	cloves garlic, chopped	3
2 tsp.	minced ginger	10 mL
2 Tbsp.	freshly squeezed lime juice	30 mL
2 Tbsp.	curry powder	30 mL
1 Tbsp.	ground cumin	15 mL
1 Tbsp.	ground turmeric	15 mL
¼ tsp.	ground cinnamon	1 mL
¼ tsp.	ground cloves	1 mL

Process yogurt, coriander seeds and cardamom pods in a food processor or blender.

Add remaining ingredients and process until smooth.

Mandarin Orange Chicken

This is the chicken dish we served at my wedding. Both have withstood the test of time.

Serves 6

2	2½-lb. (1.25-kg) fryers, quartered	2
⅓ cup	vegetable oil	75 mL
3	drops sesame oil	3
¼ cup	liquid honey	50 mL
¾ cup	tamari or soy sauce	175 mL
1	white onion, diced	1
2	cloves garlic, crushed	2
1 tsp.	minced ginger	5 mL
1 Tbsp.	Dijon mustard	15 mL
3 Tbsp.	frozen orange juice concentrate	45 mL
1 Tbsp.	cornstarch	15 mL
2 Tbsp.	kirsch liqueur	30 mL
1	8-oz. (227-mL) can Mandarin orange segments, drained	1
2 Tbsp.	toasted sesame seeds	30 mL

Make a marinade by combining oils, honey, tamari or soy sauce, onion, garlic, ginger and mustard in a large bowl. Add chicken and marinate in the refrigerator for 3 hours.

Preheat oven to 375°F (190°C).

Put chicken, skin side up, in a roasting pan. Reserve marinade.

Mix 1 cup (250 mL) reserved marinade and orange juice concentrate in a small saucepan then heat for 2–3 minutes.

Add cornstarch dissolved in 2 Tbsp. (30 mL) cold water to the hot marinade and whisk in. Simmer over low heat until sauce thickens, about 4–6 minutes.

Remove from heat and stir in kirsch.

Distribute orange segments over chicken, then pour hot marinade sauce over all.

Bake for 50 minutes, then remove pan from oven.

Sprinkle sesame seeds over chicken, return pan to oven and bake for an additional 15 minutes, until chicken is cooked thoroughly.

Transfer chicken to serving platter or individual plates.

Hoisin Glazed Chicken

Hoisin is a savory sauce made from a combination of soybeans, garlic and spices. It is often used as a condiment in the East or as part of a glaze, as in this recipe.

Serves 6

2	2½-lb. (1.25-kg) fryers, quartered	2
¾ cup	hoisin sauce	175 mL
4	cloves garlic, crushed	4
2 tsp.	minced ginger	10 mL
3 Tbsp.	ketchup	45 mL
1 tsp.	Hot Chili Oil (page 103)	5 mL
2 Tbsp.	frozen orange juice concentrate	30 mL
1 Tbsp.	Worcestershire sauce	15 mL
1 Tbsp.	dry mustard	15 mL
½–1 cup	liquid honey	125–250 mL

Put chicken, skin side down, in a roasting pan.

Make a marinade by combining remaining ingredients, except honey, in a bowl.

Cover chicken with marinade and put in the refrigerator for 4 hours.

Preheat oven to 375°F (190°C).

Leaving the marinade on the chicken, bake for 25 minutes on each side, then remove pan from oven.

Drizzle honey over chicken until chicken is completely covered. Return pan to oven and bake for an additional 15 minutes, until chicken is cooked thoroughly.

Transfer chicken to a serving platter or individual plates.

Sautéed and Stir-Fried Chicken

auté—a method of cooking quickly in fat or oil, shaking the pan and making whatever is in it *sauter* or jump, to keep it from sticking to the bottom. A skillet with a thick base for even cooking and straight sides to control the reduction of the sauce is recommended.

Stir-frying is an Asian method of cooking quickly in a special pan called a wok, which has a rounded or flat bottom and flaring sides. If you don't own a wok, a large, straight-sided, heavy skillet will do.

For both sautéeing and stir-frying, prepare all your ingredients before you begin to cook.

Sautéed Chicken Veronique

t's not necessary to use the very best wine or champagne but remember, when cooking, the finished product will ultimately reflect the quality of the ingredients.

Serves 6 to 8

1	clove garlic, minced	1
1 Tbsp.	safflower oil	15 mL
2 Tbsp.	unsalted butter	30 mL
4	whole chicken breasts, split	4
¾ cup	Chicken Stock (page 32)	175 mL
¾ cup	champagne or dry white wine	175 mL
1½ Tbsp.	finely chopped fresh tarragon	20 mL
2 tsp.	cornstarch	10 mL
	freshly ground black pepper to taste	
1 cup	seedless green grapes	250 mL
2 tsp.	finely chopped fresh chives	10 mL

Sauté garlic in oil and butter in a skillet over medium heat for 1 minute.

Place chicken breasts in skillet and sauté over medium heat until browned, about 5 minutes. Remove from skillet and set aside.

Combine chicken stock, champagne or wine and fresh tarragon, in the skillet over medium heat.

Dissolve cornstarch in 2 Tbsp. (30 mL) cold water and stir into the skillet. Bring to just under the boiling point, then reduce heat to low.

Return chicken to skillet, season with pepper, cover and simmer over low heat for 25–30 minutes, until chicken is cooked thoroughly.

Add grapes to skillet and simmer over low heat for an additional 5 minutes

Garnish with chopped chives.

Braised Chicken with Leeks

This dish is terrific on a cold night—the flavors are rich and the meal is hearty. Make sure you wash and clean the leeks thoroughly, to remove all the grit. Serve with rice and a green salad.

Serves 3 to 4

3 Tbsp.	soy sauce	45 mL
3 Tbsp.	sherry	45 mL
1	3-lb. (1.5-kg) fryer, cut into 8 pieces	1
5	leeks, white part only, washed and chopped into ½-inch (1-cm) pieces	5
½ cup	vegetable oil	125 mL
½ cup	unsalted butter	125 mL
4	green onions, rinsed and chopped	4
3 Tbsp.	minced ginger	45 mL
½ cup	Chicken Stock (page 32)	125 mL
1 Tbsp.	sugar	15 mL
2 tsp.	salt	10 mL
1 Tbsp.	cornstarch	15 mL
1 tsp.	sesame oil	5 mL

Mix soy sauce and sherry in a large bowl. Add the chicken and allow to marinate at room temperature for 1 hour.

Sauté leeks in oil and butter in a skillet over medium heat for 1 minute. Add chicken and sauté about 3 minutes.

Add green onions and ginger to the skillet and sauté over medium heat for 1 minute, then increase heat to medium-high.

Stir in chicken stock, sugar and salt and sauté over medium-high heat for 10–15 minutes, stirring constantly.

Dissolve cornstarch in 1½ Tbsp. (22 mL) cold water and stir into skillet until mixture has thickened.

Stir in sesame oil, then serve.

Fettuccine with Chicken and Pesto

All this needs to complete the meal is a tomato salad.

Serves 6 to 8

1 lb.	spinach or egg noodle fettuccine	500 g
4	whole chicken breasts, split, skinned and deboned	4
2 Tbsp.	melted butter	30 mL
1 Tbsp.	minced white onion	15 mL
3 Tbsp.	unsalted butter	45 mL
3 Tbsp.	flour	45 mL
3 cups	scalded milk	750 mL
2–3 Tbsp.	Pesto Sauce (page 65)	25–50 mL
¼ tsp.	salt	1 mL
¼ tsp.	freshly ground black pepper	1 mL
1 cup	snow peas	250 mL
¼ cup	freshly grated Parmesan cheese	50 mL
3 Tbsp.	toasted pine nuts	45 mL

Cook fettuccine al dente in a pot of boiling salted water: 3–5 minutes for fresh pasta; 5–7 minutes for dried pasta. Drain and rinse well with cold water. Drain well and set aside.

Preheat oven to 450°F (230°C).

Put chicken in a 9-inch (22-cm) square baking dish and brush with butter.

Cover dish with aluminum foil and bake for 8–10 minutes, then remove dish from oven. Allow chicken to cool, then chop into large pieces and set aside.

Sauté onion in butter in a large skillet over medium heat until soft, then reduce heat to low.

Add flour to skillet, stirring constantly with a whisk to make a roux, and cook over low heat for 3 minutes. Remove skillet from heat.

Slowly add scalded milk, stirring constantly, until mixture is thick and smooth.

Add pesto sauce, salt and pepper to skillet and blend in, then return skillet to heat and simmer over low heat for 15 minutes.

Add snow peas, chicken and fettuccine to skillet, and simmer over low heat for an additional 3 minutes.

Transfer to a serving platter or individual plates. Sprinkle with Parmesan cheese and toasted pine nuts.

Sautéed Chicken with Jalapeño Chili Peppers

erve with saffron rice and a bean salad. Serve salsa in a bowl on the side.

Serves 4 to 6

3	whole chicken breasts, split, skinned and deboned	3
2 Tbsp.	vegetable oil	30 mL
	juice of ½ lemon	
2–3	jalapeño chili peppers, finely chopped	2–3
3	cloves garlic, minced	3
½ tsp.	chili powder	2 mL
2 tsp.	ground cumin	10 mL
	pinch cayenne	
½ tsp.	salt	2 mL
1 Tbsp.	vegetable oil	15 mL
1 Tbsp.	unsalted butter	15 mL
1 Tbsp.	finely chopped fresh parsley	15 mL
1	lime, cut in 6 wedges	1

Put chicken in a 9- x 13-inch (22- x 34-cm) baking dish.

Combine 2 Tbsp. (30 mL) vegetable oil, lemon juice, jalapeños, garlic, chili powder, cumin, cayenne and salt in a small bowl. Rub into chicken and marinate chicken in the refrigerator for 3 hours.

Sauté chicken in oil and butter in a skillet over medium heat until lightly browned, about 5–6 minutes. Reduce heat to low, cover and simmer for 7 minutes until chicken is cooked thoroughly.

Garnish with chopped parsley and serve with lime wedges on the side.

Sautéed Chicken with Peanuts, Green Onions and Chili Peppers

This recipe is very fast and very easy! Serve with plain rice and stir-fried green vegetables.

Serves 6 to 8

3	large cloves garlic, minced	3
2 Tbsp.	minced ginger	30 mL
6 Tbsp.	unsalted butter	90 mL
4	whole chicken breasts, split, skinned and deboned, then cut into bite-size pieces	4
12	green onions, rinsed and chopped into 1-inch (2.5-cm) pieces	12
4	red chili peppers, seeded and minced	4
1 cup	finely chopped toasted peanuts	250 mL
2 tsp.	freshly squeezed lemon juice	10 mL

Sauté garlic and ginger in butter in a skillet over medium heat for 30 seconds.

Add chicken pieces to skillet and sauté over medium heat until chicken is cooked and color becomes opaque, about 3 minutes. Reduce heat to low, cover and simmer for 1 minute.

Increase heat to medium and add green onions and chilies to the pan. Sauté for 1 minute, stirring constantly.

Add peanuts and lemon juice and blend in, then serve.

Zimbabwe Chicken with Peanuts

ave the airfare to Zimbabwe and make this at home! Serve with rice.

Serves 3 to 4

1	3-lb. (1.5-kg) fryer, cut into 8 pieces	1
3 Tbsp.	freshly squeezed lemon juice	45 mL
1 Tbsp.	flour	15 mL
½ tsp.	salt	2 mL
2 Tbsp.	peanut oil	30 mL
2	white onions, thinly sliced	2
2 tsp.	minced ginger	10 mL
2 cups	Chicken Stock (page 32)	500 mL
½ cup	peeled, diced potatoes	125 mL
1 cup	ground toasted peanuts or crunchy peanut butter	250 mL
2 Tbsp.	tomato paste	30 mL
1 tsp.	hot pepper sauce	5 mL
1	orange, thinly sliced	1
¼ cup	shredded unsweetened coconut	50 mL

Put chicken in a 9- x 13-inch (22- x 34-cm) baking dish. Sprinkle lemon juice over chicken and marinate at room temperature for 2 hours, then pat dry.

Mix flour and salt in a small bowl, then sprinkle over chicken.

Sauté chicken in oil in a skillet over medium heat until browned, about 3–4 minutes. Remove from skillet.

Add onion and ginger to skillet and sauté over medium heat for 2 minutes, then reduce heat to low. Return chicken to skillet, add chicken stock, potatoes, ground peanuts or peanut butter, tomato paste and hot pepper sauce. Cover and simmer over low heat for 40 minutes, until chicken is cooked.

Garnish with orange slices and shredded coconut.

Sautéed Chicken in Orange-Ginger Sauce

This is wonderful on a bed of egg noodles with steamed vegetables on the side.

Serves 4

2	whole chicken breasts, split, skinned and deboned, then cut into bite-size pieces	2
3 Tbsp.	vegetable oil	45 mL
2	leeks, white part only, washed and cleaned, then julienned	2
3	green onions, rinsed and chopped	3
½ cup	freshly squeezed orange juice	125 mL
¼ cup	dry white wine	50 mL
1 Tbsp.	minced ginger	15 mL
1	firm, ripe tomato, seeded and chopped	1
	salt and freshly ground black pepper to taste	
1 cup	halved seedless green grapes	250 mL
1 Tbsp.	Cointreau	15 mL

Sauté chicken in oil in a skillet over medium heat until chicken is cooked and color becomes opaque, about 3 minutes.

Add leeks and green onions to skillet and sauté over medium heat for 1 minute.

Stir orange juice, wine, ginger and tomato into the skillet. Simmer over medium heat until liquid has reduced by half, about 4–5 minutes.

Season with salt and pepper.

Add grapes and Cointreau to skillet and heat through, then serve.

Sautéed Curried Chicken

This is a medium curry. If you like your curry hot, increase the amount of curry powder and cayenne and add some chili powder, if you like.

Serves 3 to 4

1	3-lb. (1.5-kg) fryer, cut into 8 pieces	1
1 Tbsp.	vegetable oil	15 mL
2	cloves garlic, minced	2
3 Tbsp.	curry powder	45 mL
1 tsp.	salt	5 mL
1 tsp.	freshly ground black pepper	5 mL
2 Tbsp.	vegetable oil	30 mL
2 Tbsp.	unsalted butter	30 mL
1	large white onion, thinly sliced	1
3	cloves garlic, minced	3
½	green pepper, seeded and chopped	½
2 Tbsp.	flour	30 mL
1 tsp.	minced ginger	5 mL
2 tsp.	curry powder	10 mL
1 tsp.	ground cumin	5 mL
1 tsp.	ground turmeric	5 mL
1 tsp.	cayenne	5 mL
½ tsp.	ground cinnamon	2 mL
¾ cup	Chicken Stock (page 32)	175 mL
1	firm, ripe tomato, seeded and diced	1
3 Tbsp.	golden seedless raisins	45 mL
1 Tbsp.	grated coconut	15 mL
1	bay leaf	1
2 Tbsp.	toasted grated coconut	30 mL

Put chicken in a 9- x 13-inch (22- x 34-cm) baking dish.

Combine 1 Tbsp. (15 mL) vegetable oil, 2 cloves garlic, 3 Tbsp. (45 mL) curry powder, salt and pepper in a small bowl, then rub into chicken. Let chicken sit at room temperature for 3 hours.

Sauté chicken in oil and butter in a skillet over medium heat until browned, about 3 minutes. Remove from skillet with a slotted spoon and drain on paper towels. Remove skin from chicken.

Add onion, 3 cloves garlic and green pepper to skillet and sauté over medium heat until onion is soft, about 2 minutes.

Stir in flour, ginger, curry powder, cumin, turmeric, cayenne and cinnamon and sauté over medium heat for 2 minutes.

Add chicken stock to skillet and bring to a boil, then reduce heat to low.

Return chicken to skillet, add tomato, raisins, coconut and bay leaf, cover and simmer over low heat for 30 minutes.

Remove bay leaf from skillet. Spoon into a serving dish and sprinkle with toasted grated coconut.

Bird's Nest Chicken

This sounds like a lot of work—it is, but the presentation is fabulous. Use this for special guests!

Serves 4

THE NEST:

	vegetable oil for deep frying	
3	large potatoes, peeled and grated	3
1 tsp.	salt	5 mL
½ tsp.	cornstarch	2 mL

THE CHICKEN:

2	whole chicken breasts, split, skinned and deboned, then cut into bite-size pieces	2
2 Tbsp.	vegetable oil	30 mL
1	stalk celery, sliced diagonally	1
1 cup	cleaned, sliced mushrooms	250 mL
½	green pepper, seeded and cut into cubes	½
1	clove garlic, minced	1
1 tsp.	minced ginger	5 mL
¼	head of iceberg lettuce, shredded	¼

Heat oil in a deep fryer to a temperature of 350°F (180°C).

Put potatoes in a colander and sprinkle with salt. Rinse with cold water until water runs clear.

Sprinkle potatoes with cornstarch.

Press potatoes into a 9-inch (22-cm) diameter wire strainer that has been sprayed with non-stick spray. Spray the bottom of another 9-inch (22-cm) diameter wire strainer and press on top of potatoes to make a nest.

(If you want to make individual serving nests, you can buy a set of bird's nest spoons at most gourmet cookware stores.)

Put potatoes, pressed between the two strainers, in the deep fryer and fry in hot oil until potatoes are golden brown, about 4–5 minutes. Remove strainers from deep fryer. Remove strainers from nest and set nest aside.

Stir-fry chicken in oil in a skillet or wok over medium heat until chicken is cooked and color becomes opaque, about 5–7 minutes.

Add remaining ingredients, except lettuce, and stir-fry over medium heat for 1 minute.

Spoon contents of pan into the nest and serve on a bed of shredded lettuce.

Curried Coconut Chicken with Basil and Mint

This dish is very aromatic, rich in flavor and texture. Serve on noodles with a simple green salad on the side.

Chinese curry contains coriander, cumin, cinnamon, chilies and turmeric. It is sweeter than traditional Indian curries.

Serves 4 to 6

¼ cup	vegetable oil	50 mL
3	shallots, minced	3
5	garlic cloves, minced	5
1 Tbsp.	ginger, slivered finely	15 mL
2	whole chicken breasts, split, skinned and deboned, then cut into 1- x ¼-inch (2.5- x .6-cm) strips	2
½ lb.	oyster mushrooms	250 g
½ cup	coconut milk	125 mL
¼ cup	mirin (rice wine)	50 mL
2 Tbsp.	oyster sauce	30 mL
1 Tbsp.	hoisin	15 mL
2 tsp.	Chinese curry	10 mL
2 tsp.	cornstarch	10 mL
1 tsp.	Thai chili sauce	5 mL
¼ cup	chopped mint leaves	50 mL
¼ cup	chopped basil leaves	50 mL
1	14-oz. (398-mL) can baby corn, drained and rinsed	1
1 cup	snow peas	250 mL
½ cup	roasted peanuts	125 mL

Place skillet or wok over high heat and add oil. When oil is almost smoking, add shallots, garlic and ginger and stir-fry for 10 seconds.

Add chicken to pan and stir-fry over medium heat for 1 minute, then reduce heat to low.

Add oyster mushrooms and stir-fry them for 1 minute.

Increase heat to medium and add remaining ingredients except peanuts. Stir well until mixture has thickened and chicken is cooked thoroughly, about 5 minutes.

Garnish with roasted peanuts.

Country Captain

This recipe originates with my friend John's mother, L.S. Disney. It is a mild, dry curry, reminiscent of their life in Pakistan.

Serves 3 to 4

1	3-lb. (1.5-kg) fryer, skinned, then cut into 8 pieces	1
1 tsp.	ground turmeric	5 mL
1 tsp.	cayenne	5 mL
1 tsp.	salt	5 mL
4	large white onions, thinly sliced	4
3 Tbsp.	vegetable oil	45 mL
¼ cup	yogurt	50 mL
3	green onions, rinsed and chopped	3

Put chicken in a 9- x 13-inch (22- x 34-cm) baking dish.

Mix turmeric, cayenne and salt in a small bowl. Using rubber gloves to avoid staining hands, rub into chicken and set aside.

Sauté onions in oil in a skillet over low heat until dark brown, about 10 minutes. Remove from skillet with a slotted spoon and drain on paper towels until crisp.

Increase heat to high. Sear chicken in skillet, then reduce heat to low.

Return onions to skillet, add yogurt, cover and simmer over low heat for 20–25 minutes.

Garnish with chopped green onions and serve.

Thai Chicken in Peanut Sauce

I serve this with scented white rice and a green salad. It is also wonderful as part of a Thai buffet. Make sure everything is organized before your guests arrive. At the last minute get them to help you with the actual cooking.

Serves 4

2	cloves garlic, minced	2
¼ cup	vegetable oil	50 mL
2	whole chicken breasts, split, skinned and deboned, then cut into 1- x ¼-inch (2.5 x .6-cm) strips	2
1 Tbsp.	red curry paste	15 mL
1 cup	coconut milk	250 mL
½ cup	roasted peanuts, crushed	125 mL
1 Tbsp.	oyster sauce	15 mL
8	sprigs cilantro	8
2	green onions, sliced on the diagonal	2

Stir-fry garlic in oil in a wok or skillet for 30–45 seconds over high heat.

Add chicken and stir-fry for about 3–4 minutes, until chicken becomes opaque. Remove chicken to a small bowl.

Using the same pan, add curry paste and stir over medium heat for 2 minutes.

Return chicken to the pan with coconut milk, half the crushed peanuts and oyster sauce. Simmer for 15–20 minutes, until sauce is very thick and chicken is cooked and tender.

Remove chicken to serving bowl and garnish with cilantro, green onions and remaining crushed peanuts.

Chicken with Holy Basil

Holy basil (or Thai Basil) is called grapao in Thailand. Its leaves are slightly purplish and narrower than basils we are familiar with. If you can't find it, you can substitute any sweet basil.

Serves 4

2 Tbsp.	vegetable oil	30 mL
4	cloves garlic, finely chopped	4
2	whole chicken breasts, split, skinned and deboned, then minced	2
2 Tbsp.	dark soy sauce	30 mL
4 Tbsp.	nam pla (fish sauce)	60 mL
2 tsp.	brown sugar	10 mL
50	holy basil leaves, whole	50
5	hot chilies, lightly crushed	5

Stir-fry garlic in oil in a skillet or wok over medium heat for 1 minute.

Add chicken and stir-fry for about 2 minutes, until chicken becomes opaque.

Stir in the soy sauce, fish sauce and brown sugar and mix thoroughly.

Add the basil leaves and chilies and simmer for 5 minutes.

Serve on a bed of scented rice.

Coq au Vin

E verybody has his or her favorite coq au vin recipe. Here are three of mine. Remember, making coq au vin should not be an excuse to use leftover wine that is no longer suitable for drinking. You don't want to be serving coq au vinaigrette!

Coq au Vin

prefer this simply served with broad, flat egg noodles and a tossed green salad.

Serves 4

3 Tbsp.	flour	45 mL
½ tsp.	paprika	2 mL
	pinch ground mace	
1 tsp.	salt	5 mL
1	3-lb. (1.5-kg) fryer, quartered	1
3	slices lean bacon, cut into 1-inch (2.5-cm) pieces	3
3 Tbsp.	unsalted butter	45 mL
12	pearl onions	12
1 cup	cleaned, sliced mushrooms	250 mL
1	clove garlic, minced	1
2 Tbsp.	finely chopped fresh parsley	30 mL
1	bay leaf	1
½ tsp.	dried marjoram	2 mL
½ tsp.	dried thyme	2 mL
	salt and freshly ground black pepper to taste	
¼ cup	brandy	50 mL
1 cup	dry red wine	250 mL

Mix flour, paprika, mace and salt in a bowl.

Dredge chicken in the flour mixture and set aside.

Sauté bacon in a skillet over medium-high heat until soft, then remove from skillet with a slotted spoon and drain on paper towels. Reduce heat to medium.

Add butter to skillet, then add chicken. Sauté chicken in butter and bacon fat over medium heat until browned, about 5 minutes.

Add onions, mushrooms, garlic, parsley, bay leaf, marjoram and thyme. Sauté over medium heat for 2–3 minutes.

Season with salt and pepper.

Pour brandy over the chicken and flambé.

When flame dies, add red wine to skillet, reduce heat to low, cover and simmer for 1 hour, then serve.

Coq au Vin Blanc

erve with rice or egg noodles and a light, green salad containing slices of Mandarin orange.

Serves 4 to 6

3	whole chicken breasts, split and skinned	3
2 Tbsp.	olive oil	30 mL
2 Tbsp.	unsalted butter	30 mL
1 cup	peeled, grated carrots	250 mL
1 cup	rinsed, chopped green onions	250 mL
1 cup	finely chopped fresh parsley	250 mL
1½ cups	cleaned, sliced mushrooms	375 mL
2	cloves garlic, minced	2
2 Tbsp.	olive oil	30 mL
2 Tbsp.	unsalted butter	30 mL
3 cups	dry white wine	750 mL
10	pearl onions	10
¼ tsp.	ground cloves	1 mL
1 Tbsp.	finely chopped fresh tarragon (optional)	15 mL
	salt and freshly ground black pepper to taste	
1 Tbsp.	cornstarch	15 mL

Preheat oven to 325°F (160°C).

Sauté chicken in 2 Tbsp. (30 mL) olive oil and butter in a large skillet over medium heat until browned, about 3–4 minutes. Remove from skillet with a slotted spoon and drain on paper towels.

Add carrots, green onions and parsley to skillet and sauté over medium heat for 5 minutes, then set aside.

Sauté mushrooms and garlic in 2 Tbsp. (30 mL) olive oil and butter in another skillet over medium heat for 5 minutes, then add to first skillet.

Add wine, pearl onions, cloves and tarragon to first skillet and mix together. Season with salt and pepper.

Put chicken in a 9- x 13-inch (22- x 34-cm) baking dish. Pour the skillet contents over chicken.

Bake for 1 hour, then remove dish from oven. With a slotted spoon, remove chicken and vegetables to a serving platter or individual plates.

Slowly whisk cornstarch dissolved in 3 Tbsp. (45 mL) cold water into liquid in baking dish. Cook over medium heat, stirring constantly, until mixture reaches the desired thickness. Pour over the chicken and vegetables and serve.

Chicken in Red Wine Sauce

S *erve on a bed of saffron rice with steamed zucchini or broccoli.*

Serves 4 to 6

3	whole chicken breasts, split, skinned and deboned	3
8 Tbsp.	flour	120 mL
1 tsp.	dried parsley	5 mL
1 tsp.	dried oregano	5 mL
1 tsp.	freshly ground black pepper	5 mL
1	large egg, lightly beaten	1
¾ cup	corn flake crumbs	175 mL
3 Tbsp.	olive oil	45 mL
2 Tbsp.	unsalted butter	30 mL
1 recipe	Red Wine Sauce (next page)	1 recipe

Preheat oven to 375°F (190°C).

Pound chicken breasts between two pieces of waxed paper to a thickness of ¼ inch (.6 cm).

Mix flour, parsley, oregano and pepper in a bowl.

Dredge chicken in flour mixture, then dip in egg, shaking off the excess. Use a second egg, if necessary.

Roll chicken in corn flake crumbs until chicken is completely covered.

Sauté chicken, a few pieces at a time, in oil and butter in a skillet over medium heat for 6 minutes on each side. Remove from skillet with a slotted spoon and drain on paper towels.

Put chicken in a 9- x 13-inch (22- x 34-cm) baking dish and pour Red Wine Sauce over chicken.

Bake for 20 minutes, until chicken is cooked thoroughly.

Red Wine Sauce

1	large white onion, thinly sliced	1
3–4	cloves garlic, minced	3–4
2	red peppers, seeded and julienned	2
2	green peppers, seeded and julienned	2
2	yellow peppers, seeded and julienned	2
2 Tbsp.	olive oil	30 mL
2 Tbsp.	unsalted butter	30 mL
½ cup	dry red wine	125 mL
1	28-oz. (796-mL) can peeled plum tomatoes, drained and chopped	1
¾ cup	finely chopped fresh parsley	175 mL
1 Tbsp.	dried oregano	15 mL
1 tsp.	salt	5 mL
1 tsp.	coarse black pepper	5 mL
3 Tbsp.	tomato paste	45 mL

Sauté onion, garlic and peppers in oil and butter in a large skillet over medium heat for 3 minutes.

Add dry red wine and simmer over medium heat for 2 minutes.

Add tomatoes, parsley, oregano, salt and pepper, and simmer over medium heat for 10 minutes. Remove skillet from heat and stir in tomato paste.

Casseroles

The term *casserole* is both the method of one-dish cooking and the rounded pan with one or two handles in which the cooking takes place. Casserole pans can be used on top of the stove or in the oven. Contemporary cookware is often so attractive that you can take your casserole dish from the oven and serve from it at the table. Casseroles are great for entertaining or for the busy household because they usually include both meat and vegetables in one dish.

I usually use a 2½–3 lb. (1.25–1.5 kg) fryer in casseroles. Butchers often use the terms fryer and broiler interchangeably. A broiler is a chicken up to 2½ lbs. (1.25 kg) in weight. The breast should be plump and the fat should be yellow.

Chicken, Crab and Avocado Casserole

his casserole is Hawaiian in origin. The combination of chicken, crab and avocado in a rich rosemary and sour cream sauce is sensational—but you can feel your arteries hardening. Serve on rice or egg noodles and if you're planning a dessert, stick with cookies and sorbets. You and your guests will be satiated.

Serves 4 to 6

3	whole chicken breasts, split, skinned and deboned	3
1 cup	whipping cream	250 mL
2 Tbsp.	chopped white onion	30 mL
½ cup	unsalted butter	125 mL
7 Tbsp.	flour	105 mL
1 tsp.	dried rosemary	5 mL
1 tsp.	paprika	5 mL
1 tsp.	salt	5 mL
2 cups	Chicken Stock (page 32)	500 mL
2 cups	sour cream	500 mL
1 cup	crabmeat	250 mL
1½ cups	avocado, peeled, cubed and sprinkled with freshly squeezed lemon juice	375 mL
¼ cup	fine breadcrumbs	50 mL
2 Tbsp.	melted butter	30 mL

Preheat oven to 350°F (180°C).

Put chicken in a 9-inch (22-cm) square baking dish.

Cover chicken with cream. Bake for 20–25 minutes, until chicken juices run clear (not pink) when pricked with a fork. Remove dish from oven, allow chicken to cool, then chop into bite-size pieces and set aside.

Sauté onion in butter in a large skillet over medium heat until soft, then reduce heat to low.

Add flour, rosemary, paprika and salt to above and blend in, stirring constantly for 1 minute.

Stir in chicken stock and bring to a boil, then remove skillet from heat.

Slowly stir in the sour cream.

Add crabmeat, avocado and chicken to skillet and mix together, then put in a casserole dish.

Sprinkle breadcrumbs over the casserole and drizzle melted butter over breadcrumbs.

Bake casserole uncovered for 30 minutes.

Green Enchiladas

*hanks to
Gail for
this delicious
crowd-pleaser!*

Serves 6 to 8

3	whole chicken breasts, split, skinned and deboned	3
2 Tbsp.	melted butter	30 mL
	juice of ½ lemon	
1	white onion, finely chopped	1
1	4-oz. (125-g) pkg. cream cheese	1
3 Tbsp.	vegetable oil	45 mL
12–16	corn tortillas	12–16
1 recipe	Tortilla Sauce (next page)	1 recipe
1 cup	sour cream	250 mL
4 Tbsp.	freshly grated Parmesan cheese	60 mL

Preheat oven to 450°F (230°C).

Put chicken in a 9-inch (22-cm) square baking dish and brush with butter. Sprinkle with lemon juice.

Cover dish with aluminum foil and bake for 8–10 minutes. Remove dish from oven, allow chicken to cool, then dice and put in a bowl. Reduce heat to 375°F (190°C).

Mix onion and cream cheese in with chicken.

Heat oil in a skillet over medium heat.

Dip corn tortillas in Tortilla Sauce, then fry one at a time in oil until limp, about 20 seconds. Remove from skillet with tongs and drain on paper towels.

Spread chicken mixture on each tortilla and roll up.

Put tortillas in a 9- x 13-inch (22- x 34-cm) baking dish and pour remaining sauce over top.

Spread sour cream on top of sauce.

Sprinkle with Parmesan cheese.

Bake for 15 minutes, then increase heat to broil. Broil for 2 minutes until brown on top.

Tortilla Sauce

1	10-oz. (284-mL) can Mexican green tomatoes, drained but reserve the liquid	1
6	green chili peppers, chopped	6
3	sprigs of fresh cilantro	3
1 cup	whipping cream	250 mL
1	egg, lightly beaten	1
	salt and freshly ground black pepper to taste	

Purée tomatoes, chilies and cilantro in a food processor or blender with just enough liquid from tomatoes to blend. Purée should be thick.

Mix cream and egg in a bowl, then add to above process for 1 minute.

Season with salt and pepper.

Chicken Chili

perfect for a cold winter night. Serve in a mug with some crusty bread and curl up by the fire with a good book.

Serves 4 to 6

2	large white onions, chopped	2
4	cloves garlic, minced	4
3	stalks celery, chopped	3
1	green pepper, seeded and chopped	1
3 Tbsp.	chili powder	45 mL
1 Tbsp.	ground cumin	15 mL
1 tsp.	cayenne	5 mL
3 Tbsp.	vegetable oil	45 mL
2	2½–3-lb. (1.25–1.5-kg) fryers, each cut into 8 pieces	2
1	28-oz. (796-mL) can tomatoes, drained and chopped	1
½ cup	cold water	125 mL
3 Tbsp.	brown sugar	45 mL
2 Tbsp.	vinegar	30 mL
4	dashes hot pepper sauce	4
½ tsp.	Worcestershire sauce	2 mL
1 tsp.	salt	5 mL
1 tsp.	coarse black pepper	5 mL
2 Tbsp.	tomato paste	30 mL

Sauté vegetables, chili powder, cumin and cayenne in oil in a large casserole dish over medium heat for 5 minutes.

Add chicken, a few pieces at a time, and sauté over medium heat until browned. Remove from casserole dish and set aside. Remove skin from chicken.

Add remaining ingredients, except tomato paste, to casserole dish and bring to a boil, stirring occasionally. Reduce heat to low, return chicken to casserole dish, cover and simmer over low heat for 1 hour. Blend in tomato paste before serving.

Chicken in Tarragon Mustard Sauce

All you need is some spinach fettuccine or egg noodles and a salad, and dinner is ready!

Serves 6

2	2½-lb. (1.25-kg) fryers, quartered	2
1 tsp.	salt	5 mL
	freshly ground black pepper to taste	
3 Tbsp.	vegetable oil	45 mL
3 Tbsp.	unsalted butter	45 mL
2	large white onions, chopped	2
4	large carrots, peeled and chopped	4
3	large stalks celery, chopped	3
16	mushrooms, cleaned and sliced	16
2 Tbsp.	flour	30 mL
1½ cups	Chicken Stock (page 32)	375 mL
½ cup	dry white vermouth	125 mL
2 Tbsp.	finely chopped fresh tarragon	30 mL
½ cup	whipping cream	125 mL
4 tsp.	Dijon mustard	20 mL
1 Tbsp.	finely chopped fresh parsley	15 mL

Season chicken with salt and pepper. Sauté in oil and butter in a large casserole dish over medium heat until browned, then remove with a slotted spoon and set aside. Remove skin.

Add onions, carrots, celery and mushrooms to casserole dish and sauté over medium heat for 4 minutes. Reduce heat to low. Blend in flour and simmer over low heat for 3 minutes.

Stir in chicken stock, vermouth and tarragon. Return chicken to casserole dish and bring to a boil. Then reduce heat to low, cover and simmer for 30 minutes until chicken is tender.

Mix together cream and mustard, and stir into casserole. Garnish with chopped parsley before serving.

Chicken Parmesan

This is Mama Rozzie's favorite dish. We've been enjoying it for thirty years thanks to our friend Danny Cushing.

Serves 4 to 6

1 recipe	Marinara Sauce (next page)	1 recipe
3	whole chicken breasts, split, skinned and deboned	3
8 Tbsp.	flour	120 mL
1 tsp.	dried parsley	5 mL
1 tsp.	dried oregano	5 mL
1 tsp.	freshly ground black pepper	5 mL
1	large egg, lightly beaten	1
¾ cup	corn flake crumbs	175 mL
¼ cup	vegetable oil	50 mL
2 Tbsp.	unsalted butter	30 mL
2 cups	freshly grated mozzarella cheese	500 mL
½ cup	freshly grated Parmesan cheese	125 mL

Preheat oven to 375°F (190°C).

Spread 1½ cups (375 mL) Marinara Sauce in a 9- x 13-inch (22- x 34-cm) baking dish.

Pound chicken breasts between two pieces of waxed paper until they are ¼ inch (.6 cm) thick.

Mix flour, parsley, oregano and pepper in a bowl, then dredge chicken in mixture.

Dip chicken in egg, shaking off the excess. Use a second egg if necessary.

Roll chicken in corn flake crumbs until chicken is completely covered.

Sauté chicken, a few pieces at a time, in oil and butter in a skillet over medium heat for 6 minutes on each side. Remove from skillet with a slotted spoon and set on top of the Marinara Sauce in baking dish.

Cover chicken with mozzarella and spread the remaining Marinara Sauce over chicken. Sprinkle Parmesan over all.

Bake, uncovered, for 20 minutes.

Marinara Sauce

3	cloves garlic, minced	3
¾ cup	finely chopped fresh parsley	175 mL
¼ cup	finely chopped fresh basil	50 mL
6 Tbsp.	olive oil	90 mL
3 Tbsp.	unsalted butter	45 mL
3	28-oz. (796-mL) cans peeled plum tomatoes, drained and chopped	3
2 Tbsp.	dried oregano	30 mL
1 tsp.	dried thyme	5 mL
½ tsp.	salt	2 mL
1 tsp.	freshly ground black pepper	5 mL
3 Tbsp.	tomato paste	45 mL

Prepare the marinara ahead of time and freeze it so that when you want to delight guests or family with something special, you do not have to spend the whole day in the kitchen. Marinara Sauce is also delicious with pasta for a simple meal.

Sauté garlic, parsley and basil in olive oil and butter in a large skillet over low heat for 5 minutes.

Add remaining ingredients, except tomato paste, to skillet and simmer over low heat for 30 minutes.

Add tomato paste and blend in well.

Paella

Thanks to Anne Henry for sharing this recipe from The Lazy Gourmet bistro/ catering company in Vancouver. Do not despair if you don't like seafood. Simply add more chicken to replace the mussels, prawns and clams.

Prepare everything ahead of time, so that you're ready to assemble the dish at the last minute!

Serves 6 to 8

1	3-lb. (1.5-kg) fryer, cut into 10–12 pieces	1
	salt and freshly ground black pepper to taste	
½ lb.	chorizo sausage, diced	250 g
16	large, fresh prawns, in the shell	16
6	cloves garlic, minced	6
½ cup	olive oil	125 mL
1	red pepper, seeded and julienned	1
1	green pepper, seeded and julienned	1
1	large white onion, minced	1
4	firm, ripe tomatoes, peeled, seeded and diced	4
3 cups	cooked short-grain rice	750 mL
1	48-oz. (1.36-L) can Clamato juice	1
10	small fresh clams, washed and cleaned	10
10	fresh mussels, washed and cleaned	10
1 tsp.	saffron threads	5 mL
	salt and freshly ground black pepper to taste	
1 cup	fresh shelled or frozen peas	250 mL
3–4	lemons, cut in wedges	3–4

Season chicken with salt and pepper and put in a bowl.

Add diced sausage and prawns to bowl.

Sauté garlic in oil in a large ovenproof skillet over medium heat for 1 minute. Do not burn.

Add peppers to skillet and sauté over medium heat for 2 minutes, then remove from skillet with a slotted spoon and drain on paper towels.

Sauté chicken for 3–5 minutes. Remove and sauté sausage for 2 minutes. Remove from skillet with a slotted spoon and drain on paper towels. Pour off excess oil from skillet, leaving approximately 2 Tbsp. (30 mL).

Add onion to skillet and sauté over medium heat until soft, about 1–2 minutes. Do not brown.

Stir tomatoes into skillet, then add chicken and rice.

Cook over medium heat for 1–2 minutes, stirring occasionally.

Add half the can of Clamato juice, scraping bottom of skillet, and simmer over medium heat for 5–10 minutes.

Put clams and mussels in a large pot with remaining Clamato juice and saffron. Cover pot, bring to a boil and steam clams and mussels for 5–6 minutes until their shells open. Set clams and mussels, still in shells, aside. Discard any that do not open.

Reserve cooking liquid, add to skillet and continue to simmer over medium heat for an additional 10 minutes, stirring occasionally.

Season with salt and pepper.

Preheat oven to 350°F (180°C).

Add peas to skillet, then decoratively arrange sausage, prawns, red and green peppers, clams and mussels on top of rice in skillet and continue to simmer over medium heat for an additional 5 minutes.

Cover skillet and bake for 10 minutes. Remove skillet from oven, garnish with lemon wedges and serve immediately.

Spanish Chicken Casserole

When this is ready all you need is a green salad and a bottle of white wine.

Serves 3 to 4

2 cups	uncooked rice	500 mL
2 Tbsp.	olive oil	30 mL
1	3-lb. (1.5-kg) fryer, quartered	1
¼ lb.	mushrooms, cleaned and sliced	125 g
2 Tbsp.	unsalted butter	30 mL
2	large white onions, chopped	2
1	green pepper, seeded and chopped	1
1	large clove garlic, minced	1
1	14-oz. (398-mL) can artichoke hearts, drained and quartered	1
1	4 ½-oz. (128-mL) jar pimento	1
1	28-oz. (796-mL) can peeled plum tomatoes, chopped and liquid reserved	1
2 cups	Chicken Stock (page 32)	500 mL
1	bay leaf	1
½ tsp.	dried oregano	2 mL
1 tsp.	dried thyme	5 mL
¼ tsp.	ground turmeric	1 mL
1½ tsp.	ground cumin	7 mL
½ tsp.	saffron threads	2 mL

Preheat oven to 350°F (180°C).

Sauté rice in olive oil in a skillet over medium heat for 2 minutes until golden, then spread in the bottom of a large casserole dish.

Add chicken to skillet and sauté over medium heat until browned, about 3–5 minutes, then place on top of rice.

Sauté mushrooms in butter in the same skillet over medium heat for 2–3 minutes. Remove from skillet with a slotted spoon and spread over chicken.

Add onion, green pepper and garlic to skillet and sauté over medium heat for 4–5 minutes, then spread over mushrooms.

Add artichokes to casserole dish and place pimentos over artichoke hearts.

Pour tomatoes and their liquid over all.

Add remaining ingredients and bring to a boil on top of the stove, then put casserole dish in oven. Bake, uncovered, for 1 hour. Remove bay leaf before serving.

Savory Chicken Casserole

While the chicken is cooking, prepare steamed baby potatoes with butter and parsley or simply serve with white rice.

Serves 4

1 tsp.	dry mustard	5 mL
1 tsp.	dried parsley	5 mL
½ tsp.	dried tarragon	2 mL
1 tsp.	paprika	5 mL
2 tsp.	salt	10 mL
1 tsp.	freshly ground black pepper	5 mL
1	4-lb. (2-kg) roasting chicken, cut into 8 pieces	1
3 Tbsp.	vegetable oil	45 mL
3 Tbsp.	unsalted butter	45 mL
2½ cups	Chicken Stock (page 32)	625 mL
1 cup	dry white wine	250 mL
4	carrots, peeled and chopped into 3-inch (7.5-cm) pieces	4
4	stalks celery, chopped into 3-inch (7.5-cm) pieces	4
1	bay leaf	1
4	sprigs fresh parsley	4

Mix mustard, parsley, tarragon, paprika, salt and pepper in a bowl.

Dredge chicken in the spice mixture.

Sauté chicken in oil and butter in a large casserole dish over medium heat for 2–3 minutes on each side. Remove from dish with a slotted spoon and drain on paper towels. Remove skin from chicken and return to casserole dish. Reduce heat to low.

Add remaining ingredients, except parsley, to the chicken and simmer, uncovered, over low heat for 40 minutes until chicken is tender. Remove bay leaf and garnish with parsley before serving.

North African Chicken and Chickpea Casserole

This makes a terrific meal with a simple salad, or serve with saffron rice pilaf and ratatouille for a feast.

Be sure to plan this a day ahead, so the chickpeas can soak overnight!

Serves 4 to 6

2 cups	dried chickpeas, soaked in cold water overnight, then drained	500 mL
2	whole dried red chili peppers	2
4 cups	cold water	1 L
2	2½-lb. (1.25-kg) fryers, each cut into 8 pieces	2
1	large white onion, minced	1
6	cloves garlic, minced	6
¼ cup	olive oil	50 mL
2 Tbsp.	cold water	30 mL
1 Tbsp.	ground cumin	15 mL
½ tsp.	ground cinnamon	2 mL
1 tsp.	salt	5 mL
1 tsp.	freshly ground black pepper	5 mL

Cook chickpeas and chilies in water in a large casserole dish over medium heat for 1½ hours.

Put chicken, skin side up, in a large skillet.

Combine remaining ingredients in a bowl, then pour over chicken in skillet and let sit in refrigerator for 3 hours.

Heat the skillet over medium heat and sauté chicken, onion and garlic until chicken is browned. Transfer contents of skillet to casserole dish with chickpeas and simmer, covered, over low heat for 1 hour.

Moroccan Chicken Casserole

S erve on a bed of rice. Moroccan cracked green olives marinated in garlic and olive oil may be difficult to find. You can use Sicilian olives, but increase the amount of garlic in the recipe.

Serves 6

2	2½-lb. (1.25-kg) fryers, quartered	2
3 Tbsp.	olive oil	50 mL
1	large white onion, chopped	1
2 cups	cleaned, sliced mushrooms	500 mL
2–3	cloves garlic, minced	2–3
¾ lb.	Moroccan cracked green olives	350 g
2 tsp.	ground turmeric	10 mL
¼ cup	cold water	50 mL
2	lemons, thinly sliced	2

Sauté chicken in olive oil in a large casserole dish over medium heat until browned, about 3–5 minutes, then reduce heat to low.

Add remaining ingredients and simmer, uncovered, over low heat for 35 minutes. Remove chicken from casserole dish and put on a baking sheet. Keep contents of casserole dish warm.

Preheat oven to broil.

Put baking sheet in oven, 5 inches (12.5 cm) from element, and broil until chicken is crispy, about 3–5 minutes. Remove baking sheet from oven and arrange chicken on a serving platter.

Spoon contents of casserole dish over chicken and serve.

Senegalese Chicken

Don't know how to get to Senegal? Do not despair. You can eat this and save the airfare.

Serves 3 to 4

1	3-lb. (1.5-kg) fryer, cut into 8 pieces	1
3 Tbsp.	peanut oil	45 mL
2	large white onions, chopped	2
2 cups	Chicken Stock (page 32)	500 mL
½ cup	crunchy peanut butter	125 mL
½	5½-oz. (156-mL) can tomato paste	1/2
¼ tsp.	cayenne	1 mL
½ tsp.	freshly ground black pepper	2 mL
½ cup	chopped peanuts	125 mL
2	hard-boiled eggs, chopped	2

Sauté chicken in oil in a large casserole dish over medium heat until browned, about 3–5 minutes. Remove with a slotted spoon and set aside.

Add onions to casserole dish and sauté over medium heat until soft, about 5 minutes.

Blend in chicken stock, peanut butter, tomato paste, cayenne and pepper and bring to a boil, stirring constantly until well blended, then reduce heat to low.

Return chicken to casserole dish, cover and simmer over low heat for 30 minutes, until chicken is tender.

Garnish with chopped peanuts and sliced hard-boiled eggs before serving.

Parmesan Yogurt Chicken Casserole

T his dish has just a hint of the flavor of the East to it. If you want to turn up the heat, increase the cayenne.

Serves 6

2	2½-lb. (1.25-kg) fryers, each cut into 8 pieces	2
2 Tbsp.	freshly squeezed lemon juice	30 mL
	salt and freshly ground black pepper to taste	
½ cup	yogurt	125 mL
4 Tbsp.	mayonnaise	60 mL
3	green onions, rinsed and finely chopped	3
1 Tbsp.	Dijon mustard	15 mL
1 Tbsp.	Worcestershire sauce	15 mL
1 tsp.	dried thyme	5 mL
2 tsp.	cayenne	10 mL
½ cup	freshly grated Parmesan cheese	125 mL

Preheat oven to 350°F (180°C).

Arrange chicken, skin side up, in a 9- x 13-inch (22- x 34-cm) baking dish.

Drizzle lemon juice over chicken. Season with salt and pepper.

Combine remaining ingredients, except Parmesan, in a bowl, then pour over chicken.

Bake, uncovered, for 1 hour, then remove dish from oven and increase heat to broil.

Sprinkle Parmesan over chicken, then return dish to oven and broil for 3 minutes.

Cumin Chicken

T hanks to Marilyn for this recipe—she knows how much I love cumin!

Serves 3 to 4

¾ cup	diced salami	175 mL
2 Tbsp.	vegetable oil	25 mL
1	3-lb. (1.5-kg) fryer, quartered	1
1	large white onion, chopped	1
1	clove garlic, minced	1
1 cup	uncooked rice	250 mL
1	14-oz. (398-mL) can peeled plum tomatoes, chopped and liquid reserved	1
1 cup	Chicken Stock (page 32)	250 mL
½	green pepper, seeded and chopped	½
1	bay leaf	1
1 tsp.	ground cumin	5 mL
½ tsp.	saffron threads	2 mL
½ tsp.	salt	2 mL

Preheat oven to 375°F (190°C).

Sauté salami in oil in a skillet over medium heat until crisp, about 3 minutes. Remove from skillet with a slotted spoon and place in a casserole dish. Add chicken to skillet and sauté over medium heat until browned, about 3–5 minutes. Add to casserole dish. Add onion and garlic to skillet and sauté over medium heat until onion is golden, about 5 minutes. Add to casserole dish. Add rice to skillet and sauté over medium heat until golden, about 2 minutes. Add to casserole dish.

Add tomatoes to casserole dish. Add remaining ingredients to casserole and bring to a boil, then cover and set casserole in oven. Bake for 1 hour. Remove bay leaf before serving.

Asian Chicken with Two Heads of Garlic

This recipe is not necessarily just for garlic lovers. However, if you're going to eat it, you had better make sure that everyone else does as well. It's delicious with a simple rice pilaf and steamed vegetables.

Serves 4

1	3½-lb. (1.6-kg) fryer, cut into 8 pieces	1
3 Tbsp.	oil	50 mL
2	whole heads garlic	2
¼ cup	soy sauce	50 mL
¾ cup	wine vinegar	175 mL
4 Tbsp.	honey	60 mL
2	whole dried serranno peppers, cut into pieces	2
½ cup	roasted whole peanuts	125 mL

Heat oil in a large skillet. Fry chicken pieces, browning on all sides, for about 5 minutes. Drain off excess fat.

Slice garlic into fine bits and add to skillet. Fry until garlic is soft, about 1–2 minutes.

Combine soy sauce, vinegar, honey and peppers and add to skillet. Cook until chicken is tender and sauce has thickened, about 25–30 minutes.

Garnish with peanuts and serve.

Chicken Biryani

You need a rice cooker for this recipe.

Serves 4

2	whole chicken breasts, split, skinned, deboned and cut into 1- x ¼-inch (2.5- x 6-cm) strips	2
1 cup	plain yogurt	250 mL
2 cups	white rice, uncooked	500 mL
½ cup	prepared biryani sauce	125 mL
	water	

Place all ingredients in the bowl of a rice cooker and mix together. Add enough cold water to cover all the ingredients. Turn the rice cooker on. When the rice cooker registers ready, dinner is done. Serve with naan or other Indian bread.

If you don't own a rice cooker, go right out and buy one. It makes perfect rice every time and it does all the work.

Prepared biryani sauces are available in the East Indian section of large supermarkets. It's flavored with lots of ginger, onions, coriander and saffron. If you cannot find it, keep trying. It's definitely worth the effort!

Chicken with 100 Almonds

Almonds are a
great source of
calcium. How about
a serving of this
three times a day?

Serves 4		
1	medium white onion, quartered	1
3	cloves garlic	3
1½ Tbsp.	fresh ginger	20 mL
¼ cup	vegetable oil	50 mL
1	3½-lb. (1.6-kg) chicken, skin removed and cut into 8 pieces	1
2 tsp.	red pepper flakes	10 mL
1 tsp.	salt	5 mL
½ tsp.	turmeric	2 mL
1 cup	water	250 mL
¾ cup	blanched almonds	175 mL
1 cup	coconut milk	250 mL

Place onion, garlic and ginger in the bowl of a food processor or blender, fitted with a metal blade. Mince finely using an on/off motion.

Heat vegetable oil in a large heavy skillet over high heat, until it is smoking. Add minced onion mixture, lower heat to medium, and sauté until onions become opaque, about 3–5 minutes.

Add chicken to skillet and cook for 5 minutes, browning on all sides. Discard 2 Tbsp. (30 mL) excess oil.

Add pepper flakes, salt and turmeric to skillet. Sauté until everything is reddish-brown in color.

Stir in water and simmer until chicken is tender, about 45 minutes. Skim off any excess fat.

Process almonds in a food processor or blender until smooth.

Add almond paste to skillet and simmer for 5 minutes.

Stir in coconut milk, bring to a boil and cook for 3 minutes.

Serve with egg noodles or rice.

Like all coconut-based dishes, this is very rich. It is high in fat but if you're looking for an alternative source of calcium, the almonds will do it!

Chicken Braised with Summer Vegetables

erve this on a bed of rice or noodles and dinner's ready. If you find pattypan squash, substitute it for the zucchini and squash. It will delight the eye as well as the palate.

	Serves 4	
1	3½-lb. (1.6-kg) fryer, skin removed and cut into 8 pieces	1
3 Tbsp.	flour	45 mL
1 tsp.	freshly ground black pepper	5 mL
3 Tbsp.	olive oil	45 mL
1	medium white onion, thinly sliced	1
2	cloves garlic, minced	2
1 cup	chicken broth	250 mL
1 cup	finely chopped basil	250 mL
⅛ tsp.	cayenne	.5 mL
1	medium zucchini, cut into ½-inch (1.2-cm) chunks	1
1	medium yellow squash, cut into ½-inch (1.2-cm) chunks	1
2	large tomatoes, peeled, seeded and cut into 1-inch (2.5-cm) chunks	2
3 Tbsp.	freshly squeezed lemon juice	45 mL
18	snow peas, trimmed	18
¼ cup	parsley, finely chopped	50 mL
2 Tbsp.	basil, shredded	30 mL

Mix flour and pepper in a bowl and dredge chicken pieces.

Heat olive oil in a large skillet over medium heat and brown chicken lightly on all sides, about 5 minutes. Stir in onion and garlic, cover and cook for 5 minutes.

Stir in broth, 1 cup (250 mL) chopped basil and cayenne. Cover and simmer for 20 minutes, turning chicken occasionally.

Add zucchini, squash and tomatoes. Cover and simmer for 10 minutes, stirring occasionally. Uncover and add lemon juice and snow peas. Simmer 3 minutes. Stir in parsley and basil.

Barbecued Chicken

This chapter includes a variety of marinades and sauces for you to try. When using boneless chicken, I usually cook it on the barbecue grill; otherwise I bake the chicken in the oven for 30–40 minutes before barbecuing it, to prevent drying on the grill. Take 10–15 minutes to preheat your grill when you use a gas or propane barbecue. However, if you're a '50s style barbecue fan like my husband, you'll need 30–45 minutes before the coals are ready. It's time to barbecue when the coals are coated with white ash. Knock off the ash with a long poker to release the heat inside, then put the grill 5–6 inches (12.5–15 cm) over the hot coals. Now you're ready to cook!

Herbed Chicken Kebabs

In the wintertime, you can broil the kebabs indoors. Preheat oven to broil after you have marinated the chicken. Serve on a bed of rice or empty a skewer into a pita pocket for a lunch on the run!

Serves 4

2	whole chicken breasts, split, skinned and deboned, then cut into 1-inch (2.5-cm) pieces	2
1	large white onion, minced	1
2	cloves garlic, crushed	2
½ cup	vegetable oil	125 mL
¼ cup	finely chopped fresh parsley	50 mL
¼ cup	finely chopped fresh basil	50 mL
1 Tbsp.	finely chopped fresh thyme	15 mL
1 tsp.	salt	5 mL
	freshly ground black pepper to taste	
2	white onions, cut in chunks	2
16	whole mushrooms, cleaned	16
16	cherry tomatoes, stemmed	16
2	red peppers, seeded and cut in chunks	2
2	green peppers, seeded and cut in chunks	2

Make a marinade by combining minced onion, garlic, oil, parsley, basil, thyme, salt and pepper in bowl.

Put chicken in the marinade and let sit in the refrigerator for 6–8 hours. Drain chicken, and reserve marinade for basting while the chicken is barbecuing.

Soften onions, mushrooms, tomatoes and peppers in a pot of hot water for 5 minutes, then drain and set aside.

Thread water-soaked wooden skewers with chicken and vegetables and set on an oiled barbecue, 5–6 inches (12.5–15 cm) from heat. Cook for 10 minutes on each side until chicken is cooked through, basting often with marinade.

Anita's Sister's Barbecued Chicken Kebabs

his is an excellent simple dish, using ingredients that are always available.

Serves 4

2	whole chicken breasts, split, skinned and deboned, then cut into 1-inch (2.5-cm) pieces	2
⅔ cup	vegetable oil	150 mL
½ cup	soy sauce	125 mL
¼ cup	sugar	50 mL
2 Tbsp.	freshly squeezed lemon juice	30 mL
2	white onions, cut in chunks	2
16	whole mushrooms, cleaned	16
16	cherry tomatoes, stemmed	16
3	green peppers, seeded and cut in chunks	3

Make a marinade by combining oil, soy sauce, sugar and lemon juice in a bowl.

Put chicken in the marinade and let sit at room temperature for 2 hours. Drain chicken, and reserve marinade for basting while chicken is barbecuing.

Soften vegetables in a pot of hot water for 5 minutes, then drain and set aside.

Thread water-soaked wooden skewers with chicken and vegetables and set on an oiled barbecue, 5–6 inches (12.5–15 cm) from heat. Cook for 10 minutes on each side until chicken is cooked through, basting often with marinade.

Honey-Lemon Barbecued Chicken

This one marinates overnight.

plan this dish a day ahead, so the chicken can marinate overnight. And make sure that your barbecue grill is well oiled for this recipe! If fresh tarragon is in season, substitute 2 Tbsp. (30 mL) finely chopped fresh tarragon for the 2 tsp. (10 mL) dried tarragon.

Serves 4 to 6

2	2–2½-lb. (1–1.25-kg) broilers, each cut into 8 pieces	2
2	white onions, minced	2
4	cloves garlic, crushed	4
	juice of 2 lemons	
¼ cup	liquid honey	50 mL
⅓ cup	ketchup	75 mL
2 tsp.	Dijon mustard	10 mL
2 tsp.	dried tarragon	10 mL
4	dashes hot pepper sauce	4
¼ tsp.	cayenne	1 mL
	salt and freshly ground black pepper to taste	

Make a marinade by combining all ingredients, except chicken, in a bowl.

Put chicken in marinade in a 9- x 13-inch (22- x 34-cm) baking dish, cover and refrigerate overnight.

Preheat oven to 325°F (160°C).

Leaving chicken in baking dish with marinade, prebake for 40 minutes, then set chicken on an oiled barbecue, 5–6 inches (12.5–15 cm) from heat. Cook for 10–15 minutes on each side until chicken is cooked through, basting often with marinade.

Lime Barbecued Chicken

This one marinates overnight.

The fresh, tart taste of lime does wonders for chicken! For a change, substitute ½ cup (125 mL) finely chopped fresh cilantro for the tarragon.

Serves 4 to 6

2	2–2½-lb. (1–1.25-kg) broilers, quartered	2
1	large white onion, minced	1
6	cloves garlic, minced	6
½ cup	olive oil	125 mL
½ cup	freshly squeezed lime juice	125 mL
3 Tbsp.	finely chopped fresh tarragon	45 mL
½ tsp.	hot pepper sauce	2 mL
1 tsp.	salt	5 mL
	freshly ground black pepper to taste	
3	limes, thinly sliced	3

Make a marinade by combining all ingredients, except chicken and sliced limes, in a 9- x 13-inch (22- x 34-cm) baking dish.

Put chicken in the baking dish and turn to coat well with the marinade. Cover and let sit in the refrigerator overnight.

Preheat oven to 325°F (160°C).

Leaving chicken in baking dish with marinade, prebake for 40 minutes, then set chicken on an oiled barbecue, 5–6 inches (12.5–15 cm) from heat. Cook for 10–15 minutes on one side, basting often with marinade.

Turn chicken and top each piece with lime slices. Cook for an additional 10–15 minutes until chicken is cooked through, basting often.

Grilled Citrus Chicken

esame paste is available in most Asian markets. It looks and smells a bit like peanut butter and should not be confused with tahini paste.

Serves 3 to 4

1	3-lb. (1.5-kg) fryer, cut into 8 pieces	1
4 Tbsp.	vegetable oil	60 mL
2 Tbsp.	soy sauce	30 mL
	juice of 1 lemon	
2	cloves garlic, crushed	2
	peel of 1 lemon, grated	
1 tsp.	minced ginger	5 mL
2 tsp.	sesame paste	10 mL
½ tsp.	dried thyme	2 mL
1	orange, thinly sliced	1

Make a marinade by combining all ingredients, except chicken and orange slices, in a 9- x 13-inch (22- x 34-cm) baking dish. Cover and let sit in the refrigerator for 2 hours, turning 2–3 times and basting occasionally.

Scrape marinade off and put chicken, skin side down, in a roasting pan.

Preheat oven to broil.

Broil for 12 minutes on each side, basting occasionally with marinade, then remove pan from oven.

Set chicken on an oiled barbecue, 5–6 inches (12.5–15 cm) from heat. Cook for 10–15 minutes on one side, basting often.

Turn chicken and top each piece with orange slices. Cook for an additional 10–15 minutes until chicken is cooked through, basting often.

This dish can also be finished in the oven. After broiling, reduce oven temperature to 375°F (190°C) and put orange slices on chicken. Bake for 20 minutes more, until chicken is cooked through.

Spicy Barbecued Chicken

Barbecued
chicken is a
great reminder of
summer fun. It's
terrific for casual
entertaining when
families with
children get
together because
everyone can eat
the same meal. If
you're worried
about spiciness—
eliminate the hot
pepper sauce. If
you need more
spice—double it!

Serves 4 to 6

½ cup	finely chopped white onion	125 mL
2	cloves garlic, minced	2
2 Tbsp.	vegetable oil	30 mL
¾ cup	ketchup	175 mL
⅓ cup	red wine vinegar	75 mL
1 Tbsp.	freshly squeezed lemon juice	15 mL
1 Tbsp.	Worcestershire sauce	15 mL
2 Tbsp.	brown sugar	30 mL
1 Tbsp.	Dijon mustard	15 mL
2 tsp.	ground cumin	10 mL
½ tsp.	celery seed	2 mL
1 tsp.	chili powder	5 mL
1 tsp.	hot pepper sauce	5 mL
½ tsp.	salt	2 mL
1 tsp.	freshly ground black pepper	1 mL
2	2–2½-lb. (1–1.25-kg) broilers, quartered	2

Preheat oven to 325°F (160°C).

Sauté onion and garlic in oil in a skillet over medium heat until onion is soft, about 2–3 minutes. Do not brown.

Add remaining ingredients, except chicken, to the skillet. Reduce heat to low, cover and simmer for 30 minutes, stirring occasionally.

Put chicken in a 9- x 13-inch (22- x 34-cm) baking dish and cover with half the sauce. Prebake chicken for 40 minutes, then set on an oiled barbecue, 5–6 inches (12.5–15 cm) from heat. Cook for 10–15 minutes on each side until chicken is cooked through, basting often with remaining sauce.

Tex-Mex Barbecued Chicken

E veryone has their favorite Tex-Mex barbecue sauce—this is mine! I always serve this with corn on the cob or baked potatoes and lots of homemade coleslaw! You can prepare the coleslaw while the sauce is simmering. I always garnish the coleslaw with toasted sunflower seeds.

Serves 4 to 6

1	large white onion, finely chopped	1
½ cup	unsalted butter	125 mL
½ cup	red wine vinegar	125 mL
2 Tbsp.	freshly squeezed lemon juice	30 mL
3 Tbsp.	brown sugar	45 mL
2 tsp.	dry mustard	10 mL
1 tsp.	salt	5 mL
1 tsp.	freshly ground black pepper	5 mL
2 cups	tomato sauce	500 mL
2 Tbsp.	Worcestershire sauce	30 mL
4	dashes hot pepper sauce	4
3	green chili peppers, seeded and finely chopped	3
1 tsp.	minced ginger	5 mL
¼ tsp.	ground mace	1 mL
¼ tsp.	celery seed	1 mL
2	2–2½-lb. (1–1.25-kg) broilers, quartered	2

Combine onion, butter, vinegar, lemon juice, brown sugar, mustard, salt and pepper in a saucepan and bring to a boil. Reduce heat to low and simmer for 25 minutes, stirring occasionally.

Add tomato sauce, Worcestershire sauce and hot pepper sauce and simmer over low heat for 15 minutes, stirring occasionally.

Add chilies, ginger, mace and celery seed and simmer over low heat for an additional 5 minutes, stirring occasionally. Remove saucepan from heat, allow sauce to cool, then cover and put in the refrigerator until ready to barbecue.

Preheat oven to 325°F (160°C).

Put chicken in a 9- x 13-inch (22- x 34-cm) baking dish and cover with half the sauce. Prebake chicken for 40 minutes, then set chicken on an oiled barbecue, 5–6 inches (12.5–15 cm) from heat. Cook for 10–15 minutes on each side until chicken is cooked through, basting often with remaining sauce.

Chef Pierre's Chicken Fajitas

You barbecue the chicken and your guests create their own meal!

Serves 8 to 10

5	whole chicken breasts, split, skinned and deboned	5
	or	
10	chicken thighs, skinned and deboned	10
½ cup	Salsa (page 48)	125 mL
½ cup	ketchup	125 mL
½ cup	brown sugar	125 mL
2 Tbsp.	cider vinegar	30 mL
1	clove garlic, crushed	1
4 Tbsp.	freshly squeezed lemon juice	60 mL
4 Tbsp.	freshly squeezed lime juice	60 mL
	salt and freshly ground black pepper to taste	
¼ cup	finely chopped fresh cilantro (optional)	50 mL
10	soft flour tortillas	10

TOPPINGS:

sour cream

Guacamole (page 47)

Salsa (page 48)

shredded iceberg lettuce

chopped tomato

grated cheddar cheese

chopped green onions

Make a marinade by combining salsa, ketchup, sugar, vinegar, garlic, lemon and lime juice, salt, pepper and cilantro, if desired.

Put chicken in marinade in a 9- x 13-inch (22- x 34-cm) baking dish and let sit in the refrigerator for 2 hours. Drain chicken and reserve marinade for basting while chicken is barbecuing.

Place chicken on an oiled barbecue, 5–6 inches (12.5–15 cm) from heat. Cook for 6 minutes on each side, basting often with marinade until chicken is cooked through. Remove chicken from barbecue and cut into strips.

Set out tortillas, chicken and toppings, all in separate bowls for guests to assemble.

Mexican Barbecued Chicken with Pineapple

The combination of chili and pineapple makes for a festive meal, with corn chips and coleslaw on the side.

Serves 6

1	medium pineapple, crown removed, then cut lengthwise into 8 pieces	1
¼ cup	liquid honey	50 mL
1	14-oz. (398-mL) can tomatoes, puréed	1
¼ cup	pineapple juice	50 mL
2 Tbsp.	vegetable oil	30 mL
2 Tbsp.	liquid honey	30 mL
1 Tbsp.	finely chopped fresh parsley	15 mL
1 Tbsp.	chili powder	15 mL
4	dashes hot pepper sauce	4
1 tsp.	salt	5 mL
	freshly ground black pepper to taste	
2	2½–3-lb. (1.25–1.5-kg) fryers, each cut into 8 pieces	2

Put pineapple in a 9- x 13-inch (22- x 34-cm) baking dish and brush cut surfaces with honey until thoroughly coated. Set aside.

Make a basting sauce by combining remaining ingredients, except chicken, in a bowl.

Place chicken on an oiled barbecue, 5–6 inches (12.5–15 cm) from heat. Cook for 1 hour until chicken is cooked through, turning often and basting with sauce.

After 45 minutes cooking time, add pineapple, skin side down, to barbecue and cook with chicken for the last 15 minutes. Serve chicken with pineapple on the side.

Barbecued Chicken

Italian Barbecued Chicken

This piquant barbecue sauce is quite different from the spicy North American standard. Serve with a Caesar salad and toasted garlic bread.

Serves 6

1	white onion, finely chopped	1
2	cloves garlic, minced	2
⅓ cup	finely chopped fresh parsley	75 mL
1 Tbsp.	olive oil	15 mL
1 Tbsp.	unsalted butter	15 mL
4 Tbsp.	freshly squeezed lemon juice	60 mL
1 tsp.	red wine vinegar	5 mL
1 tsp.	dried oregano	5 mL
1 Tbsp.	paprika	15 mL
½ tsp.	cayenne	2 mL
	freshly ground black pepper to taste	
2	2½-3-lb. (1.25–1.5-kg) fryers, quartered	2

Sauté onion, garlic and parsley in oil and butter in a skillet over medium heat until onion is soft and golden, about 3 minutes.

Add remaining ingredients, except chicken, to skillet. Simmer over low heat until sauce thickens, about 5 minutes, then remove from heat. Allow mixture to cool, cover and set in the refrigerator until ready to barbecue.

Preheat oven to 325°F (160°C).

Put chicken in a 9- x 13-inch (22- x 34-cm) baking dish and cover with half the sauce. Prebake for 40 minutes, then set chicken on an oiled barbecue, 5–6 inches (12.5–15 cm) from heat. Cook for 10–15 minutes on each side until chicken is cooked through, basting often with remaining sauce.

Barbecued Chicken Breasts with Kiwi Fruit

When you can't find kiwis, use mango or cantaloupe. Whatever fruit you use, your guests will go back for more sauce!

Serves 4

2	whole chicken breasts, split, skinned and deboned	2
2 Tbsp.	freshly squeezed lemon juice	25 mL
	salt and freshly ground black pepper to taste	
1 recipe	Kiwi Fruit Sauce (next page)	1 recipe

Put chicken in a 9-inch (22-cm) square baking dish.

Sprinkle lemon juice over chicken and let sit in refrigerator for 1 hour.

Season with salt and pepper.

Set chicken on an oiled barbecue, 5–6 inches (12.5–15 cm) from heat. Cook for 6–8 minutes on each side until chicken is cooked through.

Serve on a bed of rice with Kiwi Fruit Sauce.

For an added treat, try grilling mango to accompany this dish. Simply cut mango into 1/4-inch (.6-cm) thick slices, leaving skin on. Place slices on a heated, oiled grill and cook for about 2 minutes per side. Remove carefully from grill, cut off skin and brush with freshly squeezed lemon juice. This really brings out the sweet mango flavor.

Kiwi Fruit Sauce

2	kiwi fruit, cut in ¼-inch (.6-cm) slices	2
1 tsp.	unsalted butter	5 mL
⅓ cup	dry white wine	75 mL
½ tsp.	curry powder	2 mL
	salt and freshly ground black pepper to taste	
⅓ cup	unsalted butter	75 mL

Sauté kiwi in butter in a skillet over medium heat for 1 minute. Add wine, curry powder, salt and pepper and bring to a boil, then turn heat off.

Stir in butter and set aside.

Portuguese Hot Chili Barbecued Chicken Breasts

This marinade needs to sit for two days.

Because there's a lot of olive oil in the marinade, the chicken shouldn't stick to the grill. If you love hot and spicy food, add more chili peppers!

Serves 6 to 8

4	whole chicken breasts, split, skinned and deboned	4
2	red chili peppers, seeded and finely chopped	2
1	clove garlic, crushed	1
½ cup	olive oil	125 mL
½ cup	freshly squeezed lemon juice	125 mL
½	bay leaf, crumbled	½
½ tsp.	dried basil	2 mL
½ tsp.	dried thyme	2 mL
½ tsp.	dried tarragon	2 mL
½ tsp.	dried marjoram	2 mL

Make a marinade by combining all ingredients, except chicken, in a small bowl. Wear gloves while handling the hot peppers. Cover and put in the refrigerator for 2 days for flavors to blend.

Rub chicken thoroughly with marinade, then put chicken in marinade in a 9- x 13-inch (22- x 34-cm) baking dish. Let chicken marinate at room temperature for 2–3 hours.

Remove chicken from marinade, reserving marinade for basting.

Set chicken on barbecue, 5–6 inches (12.5–15 cm) from heat. Cook for 6–8 minutes on each side until chicken is cooked through, basting occasionally with marinade.

Yogurt Barbecued Chicken

Cook this over a slow fire!

This is a mildly spiced barbecue recipe. Add 1 tsp. (5 mL) curry powder to the marinade if you want to warm up the taste a bit.

Serves 4 to 6

2	2–2½-lb. (1–1.25-kg) broilers, quartered	2
1½ cups	yogurt	375 mL
6	large cloves garlic, chopped	6
4 Tbsp.	red wine vinegar	60 mL
1 cup	brown sugar	75 mL
1 Tbsp.	Worcestershire sauce	15 mL
4–6	dashes hot pepper sauce	4–6

Make a marinade by combining all ingredients, except chicken, in a blender until smooth.

Put chicken in a 9- x 13-inch (22- x 34-cm) baking dish and add the marinade, turning chicken to coat thoroughly. Let sit in the refrigerator for 3 hours.

Preheat oven to 325°F (160°C) if you prefer to prebake the chicken partially before barbecuing.

Set chicken on an oiled barbecue, skin side down, 5–6 inches (12.5–15 cm) over low heat. Cook for 30 minutes on each side, until chicken is cooked through. Alternatively, prebake the chicken for 40 minutes, then set on an oiled barbecue, skin side down, 5–6 inches (12.5–15 cm) from heat. Cook for 10–15 minutes on each side, until chicken is cooked through.

Shay, Shay Sheri's Teriyaki Barbecued Chicken

r is it Chez Chez Sheri's? Teriyaki is always a treat. I sometimes use boneless breasts and thighs and avoid the oven. Just cook for 8 minutes on each side for an easy entrée.

Serves 6 to 8

3	2–2½-lb. (1–1.25-kg) broilers, each cut into 8 pieces	3
1 cup	sherry	250 mL
1 cup	tamari or soy sauce	250 mL
6	cloves garlic, crushed	6
3 Tbsp.	minced ginger	45 mL
2 Tbsp.	toasted sesame seeds	30 mL

Make a marinade by combining sherry, tamari or soy sauce, garlic and ginger.

Put chicken in marinade in a roasting pan in the refrigerator for 3 hours.

Preheat oven to 325°F (160°C).

Leaving chicken in marinade, prebake for 40 minutes, then set chicken on an oiled barbecue, 5–6 inches (12.5–15 cm) from heat. Cook for 10–15 minutes on one side, basting often with marinade.

Turn chicken and cook for 5 minutes, basting often. Sprinkle with sesame seeds and cook for an additional 5–10 minutes, until chicken is cooked through.

Chinese Barbecued Chicken

his is a very hot marinade. If it is too spicy for you, reduce hot chili oil to 1 tsp. (5 mL). There will still be plenty of flavor!

Serves 4 to 6

2	2–2½-lb. (1–1.25-kg) broilers, quartered	2
6 Tbsp.	soy sauce	90 mL
¼ cup	hoisin sauce	50 mL
¼ cup	rice vinegar	50 mL
3 Tbsp.	liquid honey	45 mL
4	cloves garlic, crushed	4
1 tsp.	minced ginger	5 mL
1 Tbsp.	vegetable oil	15 mL
1 Tbsp.	Hot Chili Oil (page 103)	15 mL
1 tsp.	sesame oil	5 mL

Make a marinade by combining all ingredients, except chicken, in a bowl.

Put chicken in marinade in a 9- x 13-inch (22- x 34-cm) baking dish in the refrigerator for 3 hours.

Preheat oven to 325°F (160°C).

Leaving chicken in marinade, prebake for 40 minutes, then set chicken on an oiled barbecue, 5–6 inches (12.5–15 cm) from heat. Cook for 10–15 minutes on each side until chicken is cooked through, basting often with marinade.

Easy Sweet and Sour Barbecued Chicken

Barbecue sauce for the sweet tooth!

Serves 4 to 6

2	2–2½-lb. (1–1.25-kg) broilers, quartered	2
1	8-oz. (227-mL) can apricots, drained and puréed	1
¼ cup	apricot preserves	50 mL
2 Tbsp.	liquid honey	30 mL
¾ cup	ketchup	175 mL
¼ cup	red wine vinegar	50 mL
1 tsp.	Worcestershire sauce	5 mL
½ tsp.	ground cumin	2 mL
1 Tbsp.	chili powder	15 mL
¼ tsp.	ground mace	1 mL
1 tsp.	salt	5 mL

Make a marinade by combining all ingredients, except chicken, in a saucepan and bring to a boil. Reduce heat to low and simmer for 5 minutes, stirring occasionally, then remove from heat.

Put chicken in marinade in a 9- x 13-inch (22- x 34-cm) baking dish and let sit in the refrigerator for 2–3 hours.

Preheat oven to 325°F (160°C).

Leaving chicken in marinade, prebake for 40 minutes, then set chicken on an oiled barbecue, 5–6 inches (12.5–15 cm) from heat. Cook for 10–15 minutes on each side, basting often with marinade, until chicken is cooked through.

North African Barbecued Chicken

This is delicious with couscous or rice pilaf and a cucumber and green pepper salad, dressed with lime juice and olive oil. The beauty of this meal is that the salad can be made the day before and the marinade can be made in the morning. If you're having guests after work, pick up dips and pita and you're ready to party.

Serves 4 to 6

2	2–2½-lb. (1–1.25-kg) broilers, quartered	2
1 cup	freshly squeezed lemon juice	250 mL
½ cup	olive oil	125 mL
½ cup	honey	125 mL
2 tsp.	paprika	10 mL
1 Tbsp.	cumin	15 mL
2 tsp.	ground coriander seed	10 mL
½ tsp.	celery seed	2 mL
1 tsp.	salt	5 mL
2 Tbsp.	minced ginger	30 mL
¼ tsp.	nutmeg	1 mL
6	cloves garlic, finely minced	6
4	dashes hot pepper sauce	4

Preheat oven to 425°F (200°C).

Make a marinade by combining all ingredients, except chicken, in a bowl.

Put chicken in marinade in a 9- x 13-inch (22- x 34-cm) baking dish and turn to cover each piece thoroughly. Allow to sit for 2–3 hours in the refrigerator. Leaving chicken in marinade, prebake for 15 minutes.

Set chicken on an oiled barbecue 5–6 inches (12.5–15 cm) from heat. Cook for 10 to 15 minutes on each side until chicken is cooked through, basting often with remaining marinade.

Lime Cilantro Chicken with Sweet Mango Salsa

This dish is delicious with spinach orzo.

Serves 4

2	whole chicken breasts, split, skinned and deboned	2
½ cup	olive oil	125 mL
¼ cup	lime juice	50 mL
2	cloves garlic, crushed	2
⅛ tsp.	black pepper	.5 mL
3 Tbsp.	fresh cilantro leaves	45 mL
6	garlic cloves, sliced	6
¼ cup	light vegetable oil	50 mL
1 recipe	Sweet Mango Salsa (next page)	1 recipe

Make a marinade by combining olive oil, lime juice, crushed garlic and pepper in a bowl.

Put chicken breasts in marinade and refrigerate for at least 1 hour, up to 3 hours.

Set chicken breasts on an oiled barbecue, 5–6 inches (12.5–15 cm) from heat. Cook for 10 minutes on each side until chicken is cooked through, basting often with marinade.

To make crispy garlic, heat oil to medium-high heat. Add garlic slices and fry until golden brown, about 3–5 minutes.

Garnish with cilantro and drizzle with fried garlic over top.

Serve with Sweet Mango Salsa on the side.

Barbecued Chicken

Sweet Mango Salsa

1	sweet mango, peeled and seeded	1
⅛	red onion	⅛
½	bunch cilantro	½
2	plum tomatoes, diced	2
¼	lime	¼

Place mango, red onion and cilantro in a food processor or blender. Process together until it is chunky. Place in a bowl and add plum tomatoes and a squeeze of lime juice.

This is also very tasty with sea bass and salmon.

Barbecued Chicken with Norigama Sauce

This is delicious with grilled vegetables.

Norigama paste is available in specialty Japanese stores. If unavailable, Asian sesame paste (not tahini) can be substituted.

Mirin is a rice wine available in most Asian stores. If you cannot find it, substitute dry sherry.

Serves 4

2	whole chicken breasts, split, skinned and deboned	2
⅓ cup	soy sauce	75 mL
¼ cup	mirin (rice wine)	50 mL
½ tsp.	sesame oil	2 mL
1 recipe	Norigama Sauce (next page)	1 recipe
3 Tbsp.	toasted sesame seeds (page 7)	45 mL

Make a marinade by combining soy sauce, mirin and sesame oil in a bowl.

Put chicken in the marinade and refrigerate for 1 hour.

Set chicken on an oiled barbecue, 5–6 inches (12.5–15 cm) from heat. Cook for 6–8 minutes on each side, until chicken is cooked through.

Remove chicken from barbecue and cut into ¼-inch (.6-cm) slices on the diagonal. Arrange chicken on a bed of white rice, drizzle with Norigama Sauce and sprinkle with toasted sesame seeds.

Norigama Sauce

4 Tbsp.	soy sauce	60 mL
4 Tbsp.	mirin (rice wine)	60 mL
2 Tbsp.	rice vinegar	30 mL
⅓ cup	norigama paste	75 mL
2 Tbsp.	sugar	30 mL
1 Tbsp.	toasted sesame seeds (page 7)	15 mL

Place all ingredients, except sesame seeds, in a food
processor or blender and process until smooth. Stir
in toasted sesame seeds at the end.

Barbecue Sauce Sampler

Here are more barbecue sauces for you to try. Follow the cooking directions for Spicy Barbecued Chicken, page 189.

Herb–Mustard Tomato Barbecue Sauce

Makes approximately 1½ cups (375 mL)

4 Tbsp.	tomato paste	60 mL
1 Tbsp.	dried basil	15 mL
1 cup	dry mustard	250 mL
4 Tbsp.	red wine vinegar	60 mL
2 Tbsp.	freshly squeezed lemon juice	30 mL
2 Tbsp.	soy sauce	30 mL
2	cloves garlic, chopped	2
1 Tbsp.	Worcestershire sauce	15 mL
1 tsp.	salt	5 mL

Process in a food processor or blender for 1 minute, then scrape sides and process for 30 seconds. Put sauce in a sealed container in your refrigerator and allow mixture to sit for 24 hours so flavors will blend.

Barbecue Baste

Makes approximately 2–2½ cups (500–625 mL)

1 cup	chopped white onion	250 mL
2	cloves garlic, minced	2
¼ cup	vegetable oil	50 mL
1 cup	tomato sauce	250 mL
½ cup	cold water	125 mL
¼ cup	brown sugar	50 mL
¼ cup	freshly squeezed lemon juice	50 mL
3 Tbsp.	Worcestershire sauce	45 mL
2 Tbsp.	Dijon mustard	30 mL
½ tsp.	paprika	2 mL

	pinch of cayenne	
2 tsp.	salt	10 mL
½ tsp.	freshly ground black pepper	2 mL

Sauté onion and garlic in oil in a saucepan over medium heat until onion is tender.

Add to above and simmer over medium heat for 5 minutes, stirring frequently. Use immediately or let cool and store in a sealed container in your refrigerator until ready to barbecue. Will keep for 5 days in the refrigerator.

Hot Sauce

Makes approximately 1½ cups (375 mL)

½ cup	molasses	125 mL
½ cup	Dijon mustard	125 mL
½ cup	freshly squeezed lime juice	125 mL
3 Tbsp.	Worcestershire sauce	45 mL
2 tsp.	hot pepper sauce	10 mL
1 tsp.	salt	5 mL

Blend molasses and mustard in a saucepan.

Add remaining ingredients and bring to a boil, stirring constantly, then remove from heat. Use immediately or let cool and store in a sealed container in your refrigerator until ready to barbecue. Will keep for 5 days in the refrigerator.

Chicken Breast

For many health-conscious individuals, the chicken breast is the most commonly used part of the fabulous fowl. In this chapter I have chosen a selection of recipes in which only the chicken breast will do. The recipes reflect the current trend towards a greater proportion of carbohydrates to protein in menu planning. Each dish is incomplete without a pasta, couscous or rice.

Laotian Curried Chicken with Rice

This is a modified version of my favorite food in all the world. It is served at Vanipha Lanna, my favorite Thai restaurant, in Toronto. They wrap a more complicated version of this recipe in banana leaves and grill on the barbecue. On the side they serve a spicy ping gai sauce.

Kaffir lime leaves are available in most Asian markets.

Serves 4

1 Tbsp.	minced garlic	15 mL
¼ cup	vegetable oil	50 mL
1 tsp.	red curry paste	5 mL
2	whole chicken breasts, split, skinned and deboned, cut into 1- x ¼-inch (2.5- x .6-cm) strips	2
2 tsp.	Chinese curry powder	10 mL
1	red pepper, seeded, cored and diced	1
1	15-oz. (425-mL) can baby corn, drained and rinsed well	1
1 cup	snow peas, sliced in half on the diagonal	250 mL
2 Tbsp.	oyster sauce	30 mL
½ Tbsp.	lime juice	7 mL
½ tsp.	salt	2 mL
3 cups	cooked white rice	720 mL
5	kaffir lime leaves, sliced very thin	5
4	green onions, sliced very thin	4
5	sprigs cilantro	5
2 Tbsp.	fried garlic	30 mL

In a large skillet on medium-high, fry garlic in oil until brown.

Reduce heat to medium and add the red curry paste to skillet. Stir for 3 minutes, blending paste with oil and garlic. Do not burn.

Add chicken to skillet and stir-fry for 1 minute.

Sprinkle curry powder over chicken and continue to stir-fry until color turns opaque.

Add red pepper, baby corn, snow peas and oyster sauce, and stir until sauce thickens and chicken is completely cooked, about 12–15 minutes.

Remove skillet from heat and add lime juice and salt.

In a large bowl, mix together the rice, chicken and vegetables, kaffir leaves and green onion. Garnish with fresh cilantro and fried garlic.

Fried garlic is available in many Asian stores. If you want to make your own, fry slices of fresh garlic in oil until oil is absorbed and garlic is browned.

Thai Chicken with Sweet Red Pepper and Green Curry

The Thai name for green curry is gaeng keo wan. It is the hottest of the Thai curries because of the inclusion of large portions of whole, fresh green chilies.

Serves 6

2 cups	coconut milk	500 mL
3 Tbsp.	green curry paste	45 mL
3	whole chicken breasts, split, skinned and deboned, cut into 1½-inch (3.8-cm) strips	3
1 Tbsp.	nam pla (fish sauce)	15 mL
2	red peppers, cut into ½-inch (1.2-cm) strips	2
4 cups	baby spinach greens	1 L
½ cup	coconut milk	125 mL
8	sweet basil leaves	8

In a large pot, bring 2 cups (500 mL) of coconut milk to a boil. Add green curry paste, reduce heat to low and stir for about 5 minutes. Add chicken breast and fish sauce and continue stirring until chicken is cooked, about 30 minutes. Add peppers and spinach and stir until spinach has cooked, about 5 minutes.

Stir in remaining coconut milk and garnish with fresh basil leaves.

Chicken Breast with Peppercorn Sauce

This classic dish is simple to prepare and elegant to serve. It is lovely with risotto or rice and asparagus spears with lemon.

Serves 4

2	whole chicken breasts, split, skinned and deboned	2
½ tsp.	salt	2 mL
1 Tbsp.	whole white peppercorns, crushed coarsely	15 mL
2 Tbsp.	vegetable oil	30 mL
3 Tbsp.	shallots, finely chopped	45 mL
¼ cup	dry white wine	50 mL
½ cup	Chicken Stock (page 32)	125 mL
1 tsp.	tomato paste	5 mL
2 Tbsp.	butter	30 mL
2 tsp.	finely chopped tarragon	10 mL

Sprinkle chicken breasts with salt and dredge in peppercorns, pressing to make sure that they stick.

Heat oil in a large heavy skillet and add chicken (it should not overlap in skillet). Cook over low to medium heat for 5 minutes. Turn pieces over and cook an additional 5 minutes, until chicken is cooked thoroughly. Transfer chicken to a warm platter and keep warm.

In the same skillet cook shallots, stirring for 1 minute. Add wine and continue stirring until sauce is almost completely reduced, about 7–10 minutes.

Stir in stock and tomato paste.

Bring to a boil until sauce is reduced to about ⅓ cup (75 mL). Remove from heat and stir in remaining butter.

Spoon sauce over chicken and garnish with tarragon.

Jambalaya

Jambalaya is a Cajun dish. In Louisiana jambalaya usually includes bacon, ham, sausage and shrimp, but this version reflects my favorite protein... chicken!

Serves 6

2 Tbsp.	butter	30 mL
2	cloves garlic, finely chopped	2
1	white onion, chopped	1
2	stalks celery, diced	2
1	red pepper, diced	1
2	hot chili peppers, seeded and minced	2
1 Tbsp.	chili powder	15 mL
2 Tbsp.	vegetable oil	30 mL
3	whole chicken breasts, split, skinned and deboned, then cut into 1½-inch (4-cm) cubes	3
2	tomatoes, peeled, seeded and diced	2
1½ cups	long-grain rice	375 mL
½ cup	tomato juice	125 mL
2 cups	Chicken Stock (page 32)	500 mL
½ tsp.	dried thyme	2 mL
2	whole cloves	2
½ tsp.	oregano	2 mL
2	green onions, finely sliced	2
3 Tbsp.	parsley, finely chopped	45 mL

Preheat oven to 350°F (180°C).

Melt butter in a large heavy skillet over low heat. Add the garlic, onion, celery, peppers, and chili powder. Cook for 5 minutes, until soft. Transfer to a large bowl and set aside.

Increase heat to medium and add oil to skillet. Add chicken and stir until pieces are browned all over, about 5–7 minutes.

Return vegetables to skillet and add tomatoes and rice, stirring for 3 minutes.

Stir remaining ingredients, except green onions, into skillet. Bring to a boil, then cover and bake for 25 minutes, until rice is cooked. Garnish with green onions and parsley.

Nasi Goreng

This dish is very popular in Indonesia and Malaysia. Some recipes call for minced shrimp, but others call for terasi, which is a cube of dried shrimp. You can substitute pork for the beef if you prefer. In fact, you can clean out your refrigerator for this dish and use up all your leftover meat.

Serves 4

4 oz.	vegetable oil	??
2	whole chicken breasts, split, skinned and deboned, cut into 1-inch (2.5-mL) cubes	2
2	eggs	2
½ tsp.	salt	2 mL
2 Tbsp.	water	30 mL
2 Tbsp.	peanut oil	30 mL
1	terasi cube	1
2	fresh chilies, seeded and diced	2
½ tsp.	cumin	2 mL
½ tsp.	ground ginger	2 mL
1 tsp.	turmeric	5 mL
¼ tsp.	ground cinnamon	1 mL
3	garlic cloves, minced	3
1	white onion, thinly sliced	1
4 Tbsp.	vegetable oil	60 mL
½ cup	cooked shrimp, defrosted and drained in colander	125 mL
½ lb	fillet of beef, cooked and cut into thin strips	250 g
2 Tbsp.	dark soy sauce	30 mL
1 Tbsp.	ketchup	15 mL
3 cups	cooked basmati or other long-grain rice	750 mL
½ cup	green peas, cooked	125 mL
8	sprigs cilantro	8
2	green onions, sliced thinly	2

Heat oil in frying pan on medium heat and add chicken cubes. Stir-fry until color changes to completely opaque, about 5 minutes. Cover pan with lid, reduce heat to low and continue until cooked thoroughly, about 5 minutes and set aside.

Beat eggs with water and salt in a small bowl. Heat 1 Tbsp. (15 mL) oil in a skillet. Pour half of egg mixture into a non-stick frying pan. Cook until egg is firm. Prepare rest of egg mixture in same way. Cool, roll up each omelette, cut rolls into thin strips and set aside.

Place terasi, chilies, cumin, ginger, turmeric, cinnamon, garlic and onion in a food processor and grind to a paste.

Heat 4 Tbsp. (60 mL) vegetable oil in a large skillet over medium-high. Fry the paste for about 1 minute, stirring constantly. Do not burn.

Add the cooked chicken, shrimp and beef, stirring until the paste is well distributed over the meats.

Stir in the soy sauce and ketchup, then add the cooked rice and peas. Stir constantly to prevent rice from sticking, until rice is heated, about 5 minutes.

Transfer to a platter and garnish with cilantro sprigs, green onions and egg strips.

Pad Thai

This is a Thai noodle dish that children and adults alike enjoy. It's great as a meal on its own or as part of a buffet, and can be served at room temperature.

Serves 6 to 8

1	1-lb. (500-g) pkg. rice noodles	1
½ cup	vegetable oil	125 mL
8	garlic cloves, minced	8
3	whole chicken breasts, split, skinned and deboned, then cut into 1½- x ⅓-inch (3.8- x .8-cm) strips	3
4	eggs	4
1 recipe	Pad Thai Sauce (next page)	1 recipe
3 cups	bean sprouts	750 mL
8	green onions, sliced thin	8
½ cup	ground peanuts	125 mL
½ cup	cilantro leaves	125 mL
1	red pepper, halved, seeded and sliced thinly	1
2	whole limes, cut into wedges	2

Soak rice noodles in cold water, fully submerged, before you start preparing rest of recipe.

While rice noodles are soaking, heat oil in wok or large skillet over medium heat. Add garlic and sauté until browned, about 3–5 minutes.

Add chicken to skillet and sauté 5 minutes, until about half cooked.

Create a well in the bottom of the wok or skillet and add the eggs as if you were making fried eggs. Let them cook until the yolks are half set, then stir until cooked.

Add half the Pad Thai Sauce and boil on medium-high heat for about 10 minutes.

Stir noodles into skillet and continue stirring until noodles are soft, about 5–7 minutes.

Toss the bean sprouts, green onions and peanuts into the skillet and stir lightly. Transfer to a serving platter.

Garnish with cilantro, red pepper and limes.

Pad Thai Sauce

⅓ cup	water, boiled and cooled	75 mL
½ cup	white sugar	125 mL
⅓ cup	white vinegar	75 mL
2 ¼ tsp.	sea salt	20 mL
¼ cup	oyster sauce	50 mL
1 Tbsp.	lemon juice	15 mL
1 ⅛ cups	ketchup	280 mL
1 Tbsp.	soy sauce	15 mL
1 ½ tsp.	freshly ground black pepper	7 mL

Combine all the ingredients in a bowl.

Chicken Couscous

Serve on a bed of couscous with Harissa Sauce on the side (see page 85). When oranges are in season, I serve it with a salad of thinly sliced navel oranges, radishes and green onions dressed with lemon juice, sugar, olive oil, salt and pepper.

Serves 6

¼ cup	olive oil	50 mL
1 cup	celery, chopped	250 mL
2	onions, minced	2
2	whole chicken breasts, split, skinned and deboned, cut into ½-inch (1.2-cm) strips	2
2	acorn squash, skinned and cut into small chunks	2
6	cinnamon sticks	6
⅛ tsp.	cayenne	.5 mL
10	saffron threads	10
1	35-oz. (1034-mL) can plum tomatoes	1
1 cup	water	250 mL
6	carrots, cut into small chunks	6
4	parsnips, cut into small chunks	4
2	red pepper, cut into 1-inch (2.5-cm) strips	2
1	19-oz. (532-mL) can chickpeas	1
3	small zucchini, chopped	3
3 Tbsp.	fresh parsley	45 mL
3 Tbsp.	fresh cilantro	45 mL

In large skillet heat oil on medium-high. Add celery and onions and fry until brown, about 3–5 minutes. Add chicken and fry until color turns opaque, about 5 minutes. Transfer to a large pot and add the squash, cinnamon, cayenne, saffron, tomatoes, water, carrots and parsnips. Stir and bring to a boil. Reduce the heat to low and simmer until chicken is cooked, about 25 minutes. Add red pepper, chickpeas and zucchini and cook for 5 minutes. Garnish with parsley and cilantro.

Index